The Art of Metal Clay

The Art of Metal Clay

Sherri Haab

WATSON-GUPTILL PUBLICATIONS • NEW YORK

Dedication

To my husband Dan, for his help and support, and especially for the wonderful photographs; to my friends, for their contributions and encouraging words; to Mom, Dad, and Laura, for whom I am forever grateful; and to my children, Rachel, Michelle, and David, for being great helpers and for the joy they bring to life.

Acknowledgments

My thanks to Tim McCreight; CeCe Wire, executive director, PMC Guild; Jackie Truty and Patricia Walton of Art Clay World, USA; and to Mitsubishi Materials.

Unless otherwise credited, all photos in this book were taken by Dan Haab.

Title page: Bracelet by Sherri Haab. *Photo: Dan Haab*

Pages 12–13: *Silver Leaves* by Eileen Loring. *Photo: Dan Haab*

Pages 36–37: Hollow heart beads by Barbara Becker Simon. *Photo: Robert Diamante*

Senior Editor: Joy Aquilino

Editor: Jacqueline Ching

Production Manager: Ellen Greene

Cover Design: Sivan Earnest

Interior Design: Leah Lococo

The author and publisher have made reasonable efforts to ensure that the instructions given in this book are accurate and safe, however they will not be responsible for any liability incurred by readers of this book in any manner whatsoever. When using kilns and other firing devices and methods, readers are strongly cautioned to follow the manufacturers' instructions and warnings.

If you are pregnant or have any known or suspected allergies, you may want to consult a doctor about possible adverse reactions before performing any procedures outlined in this book. The techniques and materials described in this book are not intended for children.

First published in 2003 in the United States by Watson-Guptill Publications, a division of VNU Business Media, Inc.,

770 Broadway, New York, NY 10003

www.watsonguptill.com

Library of Congress Cataloging-in-Publication Data

Haab, Sherri.
 The art of metal clay / Sherri Haab.
  p. cm.
 ISBN 0-8230-0367-1
 1. Metal-work. 2. Jewelry making. 3. Precious metal clay. I. Title.
 TT213.H33 2003
 739--dc22   2003015210

This book was set in *Walbaum MT.*

Printed in Malaysia

First printing, 2003

1 2 3 4 5 6 7 8 9 / 10 09 08 07 06 05 04 03

Contents

Preface   8

Introduction   9

Part One: Metal Clay Essentials   12

Types of Metal Clay   14

    PMC® Products   14

    Art Clay® Silver Products   16

Tools and Supplies   18

Basic Techniques   20

    Working With One Ounce of Clay   20

    Keeping Metal Clay Hydrated   20

    Forming the Clay   21

    Working with Dry Clay   24

    Finishing Unfired Metal Clay   24

    Repairs   25

Firing   26

    Kilns   26

    Loading the Kiln   27

    Butane Torch-Firing   28

Finishing Fired Metal Clay   30

    Burnishing   31

    Filing and Sanding   33

    Buffing   34

    Soldering   34

    Patina on Metal Clay   34

Part Two: Metal Clay Techniques 36

Textures 38

    Creating Subtle Textures 39

    Texturing with Stamps 42

    Texture Gallery 44

Carved Metal Clay 45

    Carving on Dry Clay 46

    Carved Metal Clay Gallery 48

Working with Molds 49

    Making a Mold with Polymer Clay 50

    Two-Part Silicone Molds 53

    Making a Two-Part Mold 55

    Gallery of Molded Jewelry 59

Sculpting Metal Clay 60

    Combining Simple Shapes 61

    Sculpting Miniatures 63

    Sculpted Metal Clay Gallery 68

Beads 69

    Creating Round Beads 71

    Creating Tube Beads 73

    Creating Elaborate Beads 75

    Bead Gallery 77

Boxes and Vessels 78

    Constructing Functional Forms 79

    Forming Vessels 81

    Box and Vessel Gallery 83

Setting Stones 84

    Firing with Stones 85

    Making a Bezel for Stones 88

    Setting Pearls 90

    Stone Setting Gallery 92

Rings   93

    Creating a Simple Patterned Ring   94

    Making a Ring Bezel   97

    Ring Gallery   99

Gold Metal Clay   100

    Combining Gold and Silver   101

    Gold Metal Clay Gallery   104

Silver Metal Paper   105

    Creating Patterns with Paper Punches   106

    Shaping Metal Paper   108

    Making Beads from Scraps   111

    Silver Metal Paper Gallery   113

Epoxy Resin   114

    Using Clear Epoxy Resin   115

    Coloring Epoxy Resin   118

    Epoxy Resin Gallery   120

Polymer Clay   121

    Simulating Cloisonné   122

    Mokumé Gané Technique   126

    Applying Gold Leaf to Polymer Clay   130

    Polymer Clay Gallery   132

Glass   133

    Firing Glass with Metal Clay   135

    Glass Gallery   139

Contributing Artists   140

Resources   140

Index   143

Preface

Several years ago, I read a message board on the subject of clay on the Internet. Someone mentioned a new type of clay made of pure silver. It sounded too good to be true. How could clay be metal? I had always wanted to make gold and silver jewelry but was intimidated. Having taken a few metalworking classes, I realized there was a lot to learn, and I was not patient enough to commit to it. However, the idea that I could make something out of clay that would become metal was very appealing. I was on a mission.

I was excited to find a class introducing PMC® metal clay at Horizons craft program in Massachusetts. It was taught by jewelry artist Mary Hughes. This class was experimental in nature, as little was known about the many properties of metal clay. Not having the skills of a traditional metalsmith, I had to rely on my ceramic and polymer clay skills to form my projects.

One of the first pieces that I made was the "Artichoke Bead," a project featured in this book. When it was finished, Mary was very excited. I didn't understand why until she explained. She said that it would take a silversmith many hours of time to cut each little "petal" out of silver sheet. Each petal would then need to be soldered onto the bead to create the same kind of effect I had created for this PMC® bead. All I had done was roll out a thin sheet of clay and cut petal shapes out of it with my teardrop-shaped pattern cutter. The silver clay petals were then attached in overlapping rows to a paper core. It was pretty easy, and I had no idea I had done something impressive. That experience had me hooked.

Since then, many improvements have been made to metal clay. The clay is sold in many forms for a variety of uses. It has unique properties not seen in other mediums. Those who have always wanted to make jewelry can make something in an afternoon with little training and simple tools found around the house. Low-fire types of metal clay can be fired with inexpensive handheld torches or small kilns no bigger than a flower pot. Metal clay has applications for artists and hobbyists who work in metal, ceramics, enamel, glass, and polymer clay. It has bridged a gap between clay and metal artists that is very exciting. The best part is that making projects with metal clay is fun. I hope you will enjoy working with metal clay as much as I do.

Rings by Sherri Haab. This is a variation on the Silverware Ring project (see page 94). Use metal letter stamps instead of silverware for personalized rings. *Photo: Dan Haab*

Introduction

Metal clay is a relatively new material. It consists of microscopic precious metal particles suspended in a mix of an organic binder and water. The clay looks very much like modeling clay. It is smooth and pliable, and can be worked with your hands. Metal clay is nontoxic and safe to use. It can be stamped, textured, rolled, and shaped into jewelry, beads, vessels, and small sculptures. Once a metal clay object is fired, the binder burns away and the metal particles fuse together. The final product emerges as fine silver (.999) or gold (22K–24K). Fired metal pieces can then be finished using traditional metalworking techniques applicable to silver and gold.

The exciting thing about this new clay is that you do not need to be an experienced metalsmith to make beautiful finished silver or gold objects. If you already work with metal, this material can inspire new ideas or add dimension to your work. It provides new techniques and ways of forming metal that change the way you think about metal—possibilities you had never dreamed possible before. For the beginner or a nonmetal craftsperson, it's a way to create metal objects without having to go through the steps that are usually necessary for metalwork. Aside from being a shortcut to creating metal objects, metal clay has its own unique properties. Artists are drawn to its versatility as a medium, and many are content to work with metal clay exclusively, developing jewelry and gallery pieces that stand on their own.

Metal clay is available in many different formulas. Manufacturers offer fine silver clay, pure gold clay, and low-fire metal clays. They also offer accessories and products to accompany metal clay. Products from different brands of metal clay currently on the market can be used together in the same piece. Keep in mind that the shrinkage rates and firing temperatures need to be compatible when firing different types together.

Temptation necklace by Dawn Hale. A 24K PMC® snake with embedded ruby and sapphires, and an emerald briolette "apple." The snake is wrapped around graduated faceted ruby beads, finished with a 24K PMC® snake clasp.
Photo: Ralph Gabriner

Precious Metal Clay® was developed in Japan in 1991 by Mitsubishi Materials Corporation. In 1996, PMC® was introduced to the United States. Silver and gold metal clays were the first to be developed, followed by PMC+®, paste, slip, paper, and finally PMC3®. Mitsubishi continues to produce new PMC® products.

Art Clay® products are manufactured by Aida Chemical Industries, a company that recycles metals. In 1991 Aida Research and Development obtained the patent for the manufacturing process for the metal clay now known as Art Clay® Silver and Art Clay® Gold. Art Clay World, which distributes Art Clay® Silver in the United States, is authorized to sell Art Clay® Silver products.

Both companies offer extensive educational programs. The PMC Guild offers a newsletter, conferences, workshops, and certification programs. Art Clay® Silver also offers workshops and certification programs. They continue to develop and improve new types of metal clays and products.

The projects in this book are designed to give you a chance to explore different techniques with different types of metal clay. The projects can be used as inspiration for your own designs. Each project suggests a type of clay that has certain properties that work well for that particular project. You may find you prefer one particular clay type to another. As you begin to understand the properties of each type of clay, it is easy to make substitutions. Make sure you follow the firing instructions from the manufacturer for that type of clay.

Below: Pendant by Barbara Becker Simon. Opposite: Necklace by Kate Ferrant Richbourg.

Part One

Metal Clay Essentials

Types of Metal Clay

PMC® Products PMC®, PMC+®, and PMC3® products are manufactured by Mitsubishi Materials in Japan. Each type of clay has distinctive qualities. The project or your artistic style may dictate which clay to use.

PMC® Precious Metal Clay® is sometimes referred to as standard or original PMC®, because it was the first metal clay developed. It consists of flake-shaped particles that allow more binder to fit in between particles for excellent workability. It shrinks more than any of the other formulas because it contains more binder, so it's great to use for small projects, including charms, beads, or delicate pieces. It's easier to add lots of detail to a larger mass of clay that will shrink 25–30 percent in the firing process. This type of clay is more porous and less dense in its finished state than other types of metal clay, and therefore is not as strong as other types of metal clay. PMC® is not recommended for rings, bracelets, or other pieces that will endure lots of stress and wear.

PMC® products come in different formulas, such as PMC3®, PMC+®, Syringe Type, Sheet Type, and PMC® shown here.

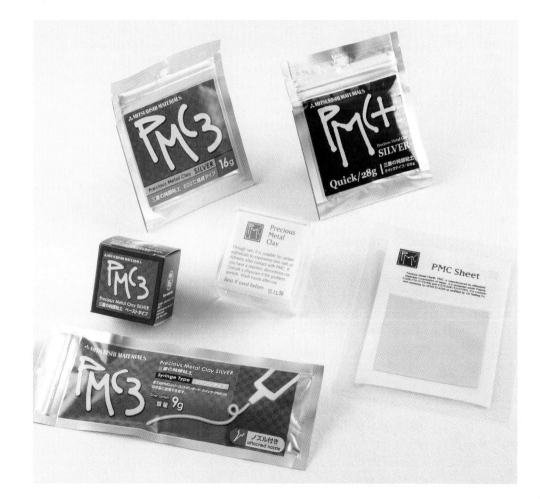

PMC+® This clay is a great all-purpose choice for most projects. It is a bit stiffer than standard PMC®, but when kneaded and kept moist, it works similarly. Its silver particles are more dense, and the final fired product is stronger. This type of clay can be fired at several different temperatures and for shorter lengths of time, which adds the advantage of firing different materials with the clay. Lower temperatures are required when firing glass, enamel, and projects made with cork clay. Firing PMC+® at lower temperatures allows these materials to be incorporated and fired with the metal clay successfully.

PMC3® PMC3® is strong and very smooth to work with. It has smaller, refined particle shapes and less binder. This makes it stronger than standard PMC®. PMC3® can be fired at lower temperatures than the other types of PMC®. It can be fired with enamel, glass, or cork clay just as PMC+® can be, however, the lowest firing temperature of 1200°F allows you to fire some gemstones that will not survive the firing temperatures required of other types of metal clay. You can also include sterling silver findings that would become brittle if fired at higher temperatures. The most exciting thing about PMC3® is that you can use small, inexpensive handheld torches or portable devices to fire the clay.

PMC3® Slip Premixed paste can be used as a glue to adhere pieces of PMC® pieces together, fill in joints, or create textures on the surface of a piece.

PMC3® Slip in a 9-gram syringe Slip is clay that has been watered down to the consistency of cream, and it is prepackaged in a ready-to-use syringe. You can use slip as a glue to attach elements of metal clay to one another. Slip can be used to fill in tiny cracks and to make fine lines on a project when using the syringe as a drawing tool.

PMC+® Paper This product is a paper-thin sheet of clay. It stays flexible and does not dry out while you are working with it. You can fold it, cut it with scissors, or punch it out with paper punches. You can also weave or braid thin strips of it. In addition, you can laminate layers of the paper to make thicker sheets of clay.

PMC® Gold Gold clay is very smooth and easy to work with. The clay is 24K gold with a rich yellow color. This clay fires at a higher temperature than the silver clays. If you combine it with silver, the gold portion of the project should be fired first and then refired at a lower temperature after the silver components are added.

Clay that comes straight out of the package is fresh and moist, and therefore easy to shape and manipulate.

Art Clay® Silver Products

Art Clay® Silver—Clay Type This clay is Art Clay® Silver's standard metal clay product. It is available in a range of packages, from large to small, with economical ones available for workshops. This clay can be fired at several temperatures, including lower firing temperatures that allow it to be used in conjunction with certain stones, glass, and cork clay.

Art Clay® Silver—Slow Dry Slow Dry clay contains a different binder than the standard Art Clay® Silver. This allows the clay to dry slowly to allow the artist more working time. It is recommended for those who live in dry climates where clay usually dries too quickly due to the lack of humidity. The clay must be thoroughly dry before firing. The manufacturer also recommends that the unfired clay projects be no more than 3mm thick so that the piece will dry properly. Scraps should not be mixed with other types of clay.

Art Clay® Silver 650 This variety is the lowest firing clay of the Art Clay® Silver types. It can be fired at low enough temperatures to embed sterling silver findings into the clay. It can be fired with dichroic glass cabochons (see pages 133–134). Some natural stones can be fired into the clay without being destroyed in the firing process. The finished metal is brighter and shrinks less than other types of metal clay.

Art Clay® Silver—Paste Type Paste Type clay has the consistency of thick cream and can be used to glue unfired pieces together. It is similar to PMC®

Art Clay® Silver products are similar to the PMC® metal clay products. Shown here are the Slow Dry, Oil Paste, Paste, Paper Type, and 650 formulations.

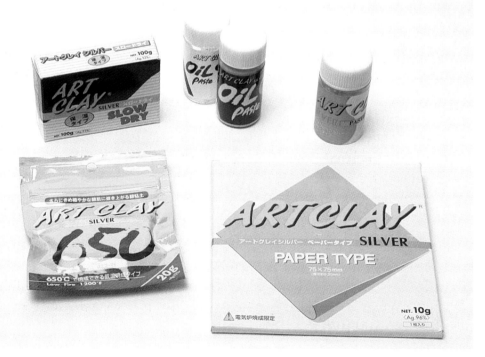

slip. You can draw patterns using the paste with a syringe. It can be painted in thin layers onto paper or leaves. After many layers have been applied, you can fire the leaves or paper and you will have a replica in silver.

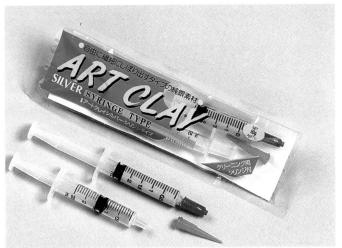

Art Clay® Silver—Oil Paste Oil Paste is formulated to stick to metal. Use this paste for broken pieces or for attaching pieces after a piece has been fired. Fire repairs or pieces made with Oil Paste at 1560°F for 10 minutes.

Art Clay® Silver—Overlay Paste Overlay Paste can be painted on or applied to glazed porcelain. The paste is water-based and will bond to the porcelain without chipping off. The paste is applied and then fired in a kiln. Ramp up the temperature to 1472°F. There is no need to hold the temperature. This product is an exciting innovation for porcelain doll painters.

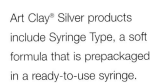

Art Clay® Silver products include Syringe Type, a soft formula that is prepackaged in a ready-to-use syringe.

Art Clay® Silver—Syringe Type This clay is a soft formula that is prepackaged in a ready-to-use syringe. This formula is thicker than slip or paste; it holds its shape when extruded. You can make fine lines of clay, surround stones, or surround forms with a lacy design using the Syringe Type clay.

Art Clay® Silver—Sheet Type Sheet Type clay provides you with a thin sheet of pre-rolled clay that is ready to use. It is useful whenever you need an even thickness of clay, for example cutting strips to make bezels. Keep this clay moist; do not confuse it with Paper Type.

Art Clay® Silver—Paper Type Paper Type clay is thin and flexible. It can be cut, punched, or folded. It can be layered to make thicker sheets. Fire it at 1472°F.

Art Clay® Gold Mold Art Clay Gold® as you would silver metal clay. It fires at a higher temperature (1814°F for 60 minutes). After firing, the gold is 22K.

The Purity of Silver and Gold

The numbers associated with silver and gold indicate how pure the metal is, with fine silver considered pure at .999. With 24 out of 24 parts being gold, 24K gold is considered pure. In comparison to fine silver, sterling silver consists of 92.5 percent silver and 7.5 percent copper, while 14K gold consists of 58.5 percent gold and other metals, such as copper and silver.

Fine silver and gold are softer than alloys such as sterling silver, and therefore, consideration should be given in designing metal clay jewelry that requires strength, such as bracelets. Sterling silver and other metals can be fired with low-fire types of metal clay when you want to include findings or other elements for strength.

Tools and Supplies

Working with metal clay requires very little space. You can set up at a kitchen table or in a studio. Keep the area neat and clean as you work, with your tools and supplies close at hand. The best part about using metal clay is that you probably already have tools from around the house or studio that will work with it. Many tools canbe substituted for those you do not own. Look around and add your own favorites to this basic list.

Working surface Styrene sheets, PVC, plastic mats, glass, laminate countertop surfaces, or Teflon sheets used for cooking make good surfaces for working with metal clay. Don't panic if the clay sticks to the work surface. Leave the clay item in place, and as it dries, it will release from the surface. You can place clay pieces onto flat, dry sponges to help air circulate for even drying.

Certain metal surfaces, such as aluminum, react with metal clay, causing the finished pieces to warp and discolor. Do not place metal clay on aluminum foil or aluminum cookie sheets, and avoid other tools with aluminum, as well.

Clay shapers (rubber-tipped tools) Clay will not collect on this tool as it will on a paintbrush. Use it to texture clay and to apply slip. Good for repairs and for blending fresh clay into seams. Fine art supply stores and polymer clay suppliers sell different shapes and sizes of clay-shaping tools.

Found objects and materials Collect fabric, lace, buttons, and other found objects to create textures on metal clay. Rubber stamps used for paper can be used to texture clay.

Mat board Strips of mat board can be used to roll even sheets of clay. Mat board is a good thickness for many projects. You can stack a few pieces for thicker sheets of clay.

Needle tool or toothpick Needle tools are used for poking holes, attaching clay, and working in small areas. Round toothpicks serve the same purpose but can be left in place and fired with the clay. This is helpful for making beads or delicate loops.

Olive oil or Badger Balm® Keep a small dish of olive oil or a solid ointment called Badger Balm® (see *Resources*) close at hand. Use a thin film of oil on your hands, tools, and work surface to keep the clay from sticking and drying out. Reapply oil as the clay starts to collect on your fingers as you work. Olive oil or balm can also be used as a mold release. Since they are made from organic ingredients, they produce less smoke than other types of oils during the firing process. Olive oil is also available in a spray at the grocery store. Use a spray for large areas such as plastic texture sheets or large rubber stamps.

Plastic wrap Wrap unused clay in plastic to keep clay fresh or to cover clay as you work to keep it from drying out.

Playing cards Stack cards for rolling varying thicknesses of clay. Use cards to move and cut clay edges also.

Roller PVC tube or acrylic rod is used to roll clay sheets. PVC tubing is available at hardware stores. It can be cut into short lengths to make rollers. Oil the roller lightly to prevent sticking.

Ruler or PMC® ruler A PMC® ruler is marked to gauge clay shrinkage, or you can use a ruler as a cutting edge.

Sanding and buffing tools Most of the same traditional tools used for silver and gold finish work are applicable to metal clay, such as the tumbler, scratch brush, needle tool, sanding papers and pads, buffing clothes, fingernail files and pumice stone.

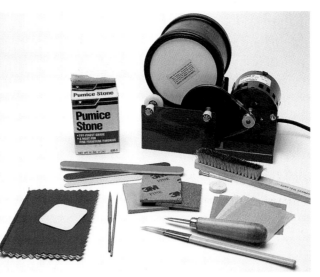

Small bottles, film canisters, and pill bottles Small containers are handy to keep extra clay in, for mixing and storing slip, and for collecting scraps of dry clay.

Small clay pattern cutters or cookie cutters Small cutters to cut small shapes of clay are available at art and crafts stores or kitchen stores. Klay Kutters, available in a variety of shapes and sizes, are manufactured by Kemper Tools. They have a plunger to push the clay out if it sticks in the cutter.

Small paintbrushes Paintbrushes are good for applying slip and water. Smooth delicate, hard-to-reach areas with a pointed brush. Wide brushes can be used to smooth large, flat areas.

Straws Plastic drinking straws or small cocktail straws cut perfect holes in metal clay. Dip the straw in olive oil to prevent sticking. Straws also make good forms for tubular shapes.

Texturing tools You can find metal- and leather-stamping tools from jewelry and leather supply stores. Knitting needles, kitchen utensils, and pieces of hard-ware also make great textures on clay.

Tissue or mat cutting blade Sharp, long blades give you a straight cutting edge. Polymer clay suppliers sell different brands of blades, including wavy shaped blades. Mat cutting blades are available at art supply stores.

Water and spray bottle Use water or distilled water in a spray bottle to mist the surface of the clay to keep it moist. A small dish or jar of water is also helpful. Dip a paintbrush or your fingers into the water to join seams or to attach pieces of fresh clay as you work.

X-Acto® knife or kitchen paring knife Use a knife to score the clay, cut strips of clay, or cut out clay shapes.

Jewelry Findings

Bead shops, craft stores, and catalogs sell a variety of findings for making jewelry. These are a few findings used in the projects throughout this book:

Jump Rings: Small metal loops that open with pliers. Use jump rings through a hole on a piece to hang the piece from a chain or wire.

Bail: A bail is a loop or connector that is placed at the top of a pendant. It's used to hang the pendant from a chain.

Ear Wires: Use jump rings or leave holes in your piece to attach purchased ear wires or earring hooks.

Head and Eye Pins: A head pin is a short wire with a ball or flat pad on one end. You can hang a bead on a head pin and then coil the top to make a loop for hanging. An eye pin is similar, except it has a loop on the bottom. This allows you to hang another piece or bead to dangle from the loop. It can also be used to make a series of connections to link pieces together, for example, a bracelet made with a series of pieces connected in a row.

Sterling Silver Wire: Wire can be twisted or wrapped to use as a decorative element or to make connections and findings.

Pin Backs: Purchased pin backs can be glued to the back of a pin made from metal clay with epoxy.

Basic Techniques

Working with One Ounce of Clay

In my workshops, I've noted that students are always amazed at how far an ounce of clay goes. When they see the small lump of clay in front of them, some are afraid to get started and others fret about making just the right thing with this tiny, "precious" lump of clay. I remind them that one ounce of clay goes a long way, and that if they make a mistake, they can always wad it back up and start over.

A one-ounce lump of clay is more than enough to make a bracelet full of charms, with matching earrings, plus pendants and beads, as shown here.

Keeping Metal Clay Hydrated

After you open a package of metal clay, pinch off a small amount to become familiar with the material. Keep the rest of the clay wrapped up in a sealed package to prevent drying. You will want to pace yourself and control the drying of the clay as you progress through a project. There are different stages of workability as the clay goes from fresh moist clay to bone-dry and everything in between. Some people are nervous when they first open the clay and fear it will dry out too quickly as they are working on a project. You can relax if you attend to your clay, keeping it moist and getting used to different stages of drying as it relates to your climate.

There are instances when you want to speed up drying time, and other occasions when you need the clay to stay moist and flexible as you work. The great part is that dried clay can be rehydrated, and scraps can be used to make slip. Metal clay can be recycled in this way, and nothing is lost or wasted.

There are several ways to keep clay hydrated: You can periodically mist the clay using a spray bottle, or you can sprinkle water on the clay. Remove small pieces of clay as you work, keeping the rest in plastic wrap inside a sealed container with a small damp sponge to prevent it from drying out. If the clay becomes too dry, add water drops and leave it wrapped up to rehydrate for a few hours or overnight. Bone-dry clay may take longer, but it can still be reconditioned into soft clay. Olive oil or Badger Balm® also helps to keep your hands and clay from drying out while you work.

Forming the Clay

Working with Fresh Wet Clay Fresh, moist clay is easy to shape and manipulate. Make delicate components such as loops, braids, and fine details at this stage, while the clay is soft and flexible. Pieces of wet clay can be attached to one another simply by applying water and adhering the clay elements together. Slip can also be used sparingly to wet clay, but be cautious: Cleaning up slip around joints is tricky on fresh clay, as the clay piece will be marred or lose texture if the clay is too wet. With a little practice, you can learn to judge when it is best to attach elements of clay or to use slip.

Rolling Sheets of Metal Clay Place a lump of metal clay on your work surface and use a roller to roll the clay into a sheet. If the clay sticks, rub a small amount of olive oil or balm on the work surface and the roller. If the clay cracks and splits, it may be too dry. Mist the surface with water, wait a minute, and try rolling the clay again. If you see any air bubbles form as you roll out the clay, pierce them with a needle tool or toothpick, and smooth the clay with your roller or fingers. Many of the projects in this book were made with sheets of rolled clay. The following are two methods of rolling out an even thickness of clay:

Roll the clay between two strips of mat board to get a thickness of about 1.5mm. This thickness is sturdy enough for most metal clay projects, such as pendants, rings, or the wall of a vessel or box. From there, you can roll the clay to a thinner sheet by eye.

Alternatively, use playing cards stacked for varying thicknesses, a clever method developed by Tim McCreight. Place the clay between the stacks: 5–6 cards for thicker sheets, 4 cards for medium thickness, and 2–3 cards for thin sheets.

Making Ropes and Loops Use fresh clay to make ropes or "snakes" out of clay. Thick ropes or snakes make sturdy loops or bails for pendants, and fine ropes can be used as decorative elements. To roll a snake of clay, pinch off a small amount of clay and use both hands to roll the clay on your work surface with your fingertips.

As you roll, move along the length of the snake, applying even pressure with your fingers for a uniform thickness. As you apply downward pressure, push or coax the clay away from the center outward to lengthen it. If the rope gets too long to manage, cut it into shorter pieces and continue rolling until you have the thickness you need.

Spray the clay with water as needed to keep it moist. If you leave a rope of clay while working on another element, keep it covered with a wet paper towel or plastic wrap.

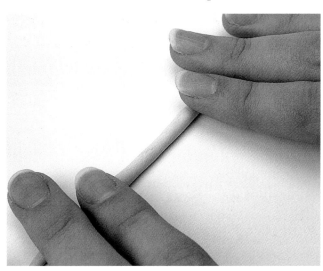

With the ropes of clay, you can make loops or hooks to attach to clay projects. Pendant bails or rings can be attached before firing. Soldering is not required. In fact, you may want to skip soldering altogether, because fired metal clay is porous and soaks up solder.

To make a loop or small ring of clay, form a small thin rope of clay into a circle. Cut the ends cleanly to make a butt joint. Press the ends together with water to seal. Let the loop dry and attach to the unfired metal clay with thick slip. More slip applied to the piece as it dries will ensure a secure bond.

To get a uniform thickness, use both hands to apply even pressure.

Making Slip Dry bits of clay or unfired clay shavings can be added to a small jar to make slip. Slip is clay that has been watered down to the consistency of cream. Slip acts as a "glue" to attach either wet or dry clay elements to each other. You can buy premixed slip in paste form from metal clay manufacturers or you can make your own. To make your own, mix clay with distilled water and a few drops of vinegar in a small bottle or lidded container. The distilled water and vinegar keep mold from growing on the clay. If you're in a hurry, you can mix slip right on your work surface with moist clay and water. Use a clay shaper tool to make a smooth paste or slip. Mark your slip jars to remember which type of clay they contain. Always keep slip made with oil paste separate.

Syringe Type Clay A syringe is perfect for working with either soft clay or slip, both of which are available in preloaded syringes. Syringe Type clay is a soft clay and is perfect for making fine lines and ropes of clay. This is helpful when you need to cover or surround a large area with a fine rope, as the syringe offers more control than making a skinny rope by hand.

Syringe slip is helpful to use when applying slip to joints. It's less messy and easier to apply in tight areas or cracks. You can make your own syringe clay or slip, however it is more challenging to achieve the correct consistency.

Keep the tip of the syringe submerged in a small jar of water to keep unused clay hydrated. Florist's vials with a rubber top used for a single rose are perfect for clay syringe storage. You will want to keep the clay hydrated or clean it out after each use, or it is difficult to remover the clay from the syringe. If the clay dries, you can soak the syringe to loosen the dried clay.

Texture on Metal Clay One of the best features of the clay is that it is so refined that it will pick up subtle details from textured objects. There is no end to what you can use to texture clay. You can use fabric, lace, rubber stamps, and metal or leather tools. Even found objects around the house or objects found in nature provide plenty of sources for great textures. Olive oil can be used to keep the tools or material from sticking to the clay.

Adding Elements As metal clay starts to dry it will hold its shape. When it is stiff enough to handle you can add fresh clay attachments to the clay form with slip and water. At this stage, there is still enough moisture in the clay to make the attachments adhere easily without ruining the shape of the clay. It is helpful to score or stipple the pieces that will be joined together with a knife before adding slip to bond the pieces. This will help the slip to stick to both pieces for a tight bond.

Small pieces of rolled paper, cardboard, or straws can be used to prop and support the clay as it dries. Remember, you can always slow the drying process by adding a few drops of water and letting the clay absorb the water for a few minutes to allow more working time. It won't take long to get a feel for the proper timing necessary to move back and forth between the different stages of wet and dry clay.

Three-dimensional forms, such as beads, can be propped up to dry with toothpicks or skewers stuck into a styrofoam block or in a cup filled with sand.

Syringe Type clay is applied to a bead core to make a lace pattern for a hollow bead.

Textures from a variety of found objects may be transferred to metal clay.

Working with Dry Clay

The stage between moist and flexible clay and bone-dry clay is called leather-hard. The piece looks and feels dry but has enough moisture to join pieces together. To join two leather-hard pieces of clay, score both pieces and add slip to glue the pieces together. This is also the stage at which you can carve designs into the dry clay with a sharp V-shaped carving tool to make crisp lines.

Clay that is completely dry is called bone-dry. Care should be taken while handling bone-dry clay at this stage. The clay appears to be strong, but can break if you apply too much pressure or stress to a piece. Elements can still be added or patched with raw clay and slip, but several applications may be necessary to create a strong connection.

With a pin vise, you can refine or enlarge holes (used to thread a chain through) in a leather-hard piece. A pin vise is a small tool to hold a drill bit that can drill a hole into the clay. Be careful not to make the hole too close to the edge of the clay or the clay will split. Smooth the surface with a small amount of water on a sponge or paintbrush to remove any surface irregularities as a final step in working with bone-dry clay.

You can tell that metal clay is dry by the way it looks and feels. Dry clay will be lighter in color as the moisture leaves. Damp clay is cool to the touch. Small, thin pieces will dry quickly (approximately 30 minutes). The type of clay used, the thickness of the clay, the climate, and the humidity all determine the length of time needed to dry metal clay.

Finished pieces will dry quickly and evenly on a wire rack or on a dry sponge, which helps air circulation. Larger pieces of clay can take a few hours or more to dry. If you want to make sure a thick piece of clay is bone-dry, you can leave it overnight or speed the drying time with heat. To speed drying, use a hair dryer, food dehydrator, or coffee mug warming plate. If pieces warp as they dry, you can bend or flatten the metal after the piece is fired.

It's best to let finished pieces dry thoroughly before firing. If any moisture remains in the clay during firing, steam will expand and escape causing cracks in the clay. Hidden air bubbles trap steam, which could burst though the piece as it escapes from wet clay.

A pin vise with a small drill bit can be used to drill a hole into the clay.

Finishing Unfired Metal Clay

Use sanding papers or nail files to sand edges and finish the metal clay piece as much as possible before firing. Cleaning up the piece at this stage saves time and effort in the finishing process after the piece is fired. Dry unfired clay is fragile at this stage. Take care to hold and support the piece so that you are not causing stress that could break it.

Before beginning, determine how much needs to be refined. Fine sanding papers are usually sufficient. Nail files are small and work very well to bevel edges of rings or to sand the edges of a pendant. For tight spots, use fine sanding cloths cut into small pieces to sand around small details.

After you have sanded a piece, you can smooth any hard-to-reach areas with a small paintbrush and water. Be careful about removing textures with water; only a small amount of water is needed to soften edges. Damp cosmetic sponges work well to smooth the dried clay.

Repairs   Unfired and fired clay can be repaired if broken. Unfired clay can be repaired before firing the piece. Brush water onto the broken unfired pieces and then apply thin slip. Press the broken pieces together, and let the repaired clay dry. Carefully add more slip to fill in any cracks that appear while it dries. Smooth the piece with water and thin slip if needed until the crack is no longer visible. Handle the piece carefully until it is refired.

Fired metal objects sometimes break due to a poor attachment or underfiring. Sometimes a stress crack forms at a seam during the firing process. Fired metal clay can be repaired using fresh clay and thick slip or paste and then refiring. Sometimes it's tricky to get slip or paste to stick to the metal. You can apply a thick layer to hold the pieces together and then refine the piece after firing, with a metal file. Art Clay® Silver makes an oil-based paste that works well to join fired pieces. Paste can also be used to change or add elements to fired metal clay objects.

Unfired clay can be repaired before firing by brushing water and thin slip onto the broken pieces, and then pressing them together to dry.

While the piece is drying, you can add more slip to fill in any cracks that appear.

Both buttons were torch-fired. The one on the bottom was overheated. Notice how the detail of the moon was lost as the silver started to melt.

Firing

There are several methods for firing metal clay. A small kiln, torch, or other firing device reaches high enough temperatures. Anyone who sells metal clay supplies can help you with the right firing appliance. Firing equipment is also available through jewelry and glass suppliers.

Metal clay needs to be fired at a high enough temperature and held long enough to fuse the metal particles properly. Underfired pieces will be brittle and snap like chalk. Overheating will melt the metal. Do not fire the metal clays above the melting temperatures of 1762°F for fine silver, 1945°F for 24K gold and 1931°F for 22K gold. Metal will melt into a pool in the kiln if the metal is overheated. You can see metal start to shimmer like mercury if you are overheating while torch-firing.

Each type of clay has different firing possibilities. Refer to the firing chart (see page 29), and make sure you fire your metal clay pieces correctly. The firing times listed on the firing charts are minimums. It will not harm the metal to fire for longer than is suggested. Doing so allows you to fire different types of clays together. However, if a project requires a lower firing temperature—because it contains a stone or cork clay, for example—always fire the whole thing at that temperature.

Kilns

Kilns have been developed especially for firing metal clay. These kilns are small and have programmable time and temperature controls built in. A small enameling kiln outfitted with a pyrometer can also be used to kiln-fire the clay. Large kilns, even if they have a controller, fluctuate quite a bit in temperature and pose a risk of under- or overfiring metal clay. The temperature and time need to be consistent for metal clay to fuse properly.

Small portable firing devices such as the Hot Pot™ or the Ultra Lite Beehive Kiln are inexpensive alternatives to a full-sized electronic kiln. You can fire a few pieces at a time very quickly. These are great if you do not want to invest in a full-sized kiln.

Electric kilns especially made for firing metal clay can be programmed for temperature and time. This feature guards against overheating and other problems during firing.

Kiln Safety

Follow these safety tips:
- *Read the kiln manufacturer's instructions carefully before using your kiln.*
- *Do not fire the kiln hotter than it is recommended for the metal clay.*
- *Do not leave the kiln unattended while firing.*
- *Do not touch the sides of the kiln while it is heated.*
- *Fire in a well-ventilated area.*
- *Dangerous voltage: Do not bring anything into contact with the heating elements. Unplug the kiln after firing.*
- *Wear safety glasses when opening the door of the hot kiln.*
- *Always fire your metal clay items on a kiln shelf, not the kiln floor.*

Loading the Kiln

Prepare the metal clay pieces for firing. Make sure that everything that is being fired together is compatible temperature-wise. Use the lowest temperature for a longer length of time if you are combining different types of clay in the batch or using materials, such as cork clay, which if overheated can melt metal clay. Firing accessories are available from metal clay suppliers. Set the clay pieces on a kiln shelf or a hard Solderite™ pad. Arrange the pieces close together but not touching. Round or shaped pieces need to be supported with refractory ceramic fiber, sometimes known as "fiber blanket," "fiber cloth," or "doll prop." It is used for making porcelain dolls and is available in ceramic stores.

You can use small pieces of kiln brick or kiln shelf to stack multiple shelves in the kiln. Place the same-sized blocks on each corner for stability as you stack the shelves. Load the kiln with the shelves of metal clay pieces. Make sure that nothing is touching the thermocouple (a small probe on the back wall of the kiln that controls the temperature).

Some artists use other materials for supporting metal clay during firing. Small terra-cotta pots filled with vermiculite, or Alumina Hydrate can be used to support round or curved objects. It can be used on a kiln shelf in thin layers to fire rings or enameled metal clay pieces to prevent sticking. *Alumina Hydrate is very fine powder, and you must wear a dust mask or respirator while using it. It can damage your lungs if you breathe the dust.*

Creative Paperclay® is another product helpful in supporting the clay while it fires. It is made out of volcanic ash and survives the firings intact. You can shape wet metal clay on Creative Paperclay® forms to make slumped or domed shapes. It can also be used inside rings and beads to hold the shape of the clay while firing.

Load the kiln and set the controls for the proper time and temperature needed to fire the metal clay. After the firing, unplug the kiln and let it cool down. You can let the kiln cool slowly or open the door to cool it down quickly.

Remove the shelves with oven mitts or tongs. Pieces *without* stones or inclusions can be quenched in water to cool. Stones may shatter if cooled too quickly, so let these cool slowly at room temperature.

The Ultra Lite Beehive Kiln heats quickly and evenly, providing the ideal temperature for firing metal clay. The pieces should be completely dry before firing.

Round or shaped pieces need to be placed on extra support to retain their forms. As shown here, flat pieces are laid directly on the kiln shelf, while a fiber blanket, or "doll prop," is used to cradle the round beads.

Butane Torch-Firing

Low-fire metal clay types can be fired with a small handheld torch instead of a kiln. These are the same kind of torches used to caramelize sugar for crème brûlée. Butane fuel for the torch is available at grocery or variety stores. It's the fuel used to fill cigarette lighters. Torch-firing works for small pieces (smaller than a silver dollar and/or projects made with less than 25 grams of metal clay). You must also use one of the low-firing clay types for torch-firing. PMC3®, Art Clay® Silver, and Art Clay® Silver 650 work well for torch-firing. To fire metal clay with a torch, follow these steps:

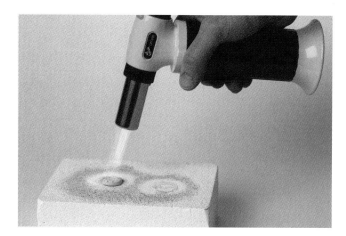

1 It is critical that your piece is completely dry before firing with a torch. Place it on a firebrick or soldering block. Make sure you're working on a heat-proof table, away from anything combustible. If a metal clay piece contains a stone, place it face down. Only use stones that are strong enough to withstand high temperatures. Fill the torch with butane.

2 Ignite the torch and hold it over the piece at a very close range. Keep the torch moving slowly over the piece, holding it about 1.5 inches away. A small flame and smoke will briefly appear as the binder burns out.

3 Keep the torch moving and watch as the piece glows red-orange. It's easier to see the orange color in a darker room, away from bright light or sunlight. Keep the metal glowing with even heat for proper fusing, and at the same time avoid melting the piece, which can happen quickly if you are not paying attention.

4 As soon as the piece glows red-orange, start timing, at least 1.5–2 minutes for a small piece. Large pieces can take up to 5 minutes, but it doesn't hurt to fire any piece longer. If the piece starts to look shiny, the silver is melting. Quickly pull the torch back. Continue firing, adjusting the torch distance as needed. After firing, turn off the torch and let the piece cool. Finish the piece as directed.

Precious Metal Clay® Kiln Firing Chart

Clay Type/Properties	Firing temp/ minimum time	Recommended firing method	Shrinkage
PMC® Good for small projects when shrinkage is desired, very smooth clay, good for charms, pendants, small sculptures	1650°F for 2 hours	Kiln	25–30%
PMC+® Strong clay, good for bracelets, earrings, rings, pins, vessels, beads, enameling	1650°F for 10 min. 1560°F for 20 min. 1470°F for 30 min.	Kiln	10–15%
PMC3® Stones such as garnets, moonstones, and hematite. Can be fired with glass and sterling silver findings.	1290°F for 10 min. 1200°F for 20 min. 1110°F for 30 min.	Kiln or torch (see instructions on page 28 for torch-firing)	10–12%
PMC GOLD® 24K Pendants, charms, earrings	1830°F for 2 hours	Kiln	25–30%

Art Clay® Kiln Firing Chart

Clay Type/Properties	Firing temp/ minimum time	Recommended firing method	Shrinkage
Art Clay® Silver-Clay Type Strong all purpose metal clay, good for pins, pendants, sculpted forms, beads	1600°F for 10 min. 1560°F for 20 min. 1472°F for 30 min.	Kiln or Torch (see instructions on page 28 for torch-firing)	8-12%
Art Clay® Silver-Slow Dry Good for rings and detailed pieces, helpful in dry climates, allows longer working time	1600°F for 10 min. 1560°F for 20 min. 1472°F for 30 min	Kiln or Torch (see instructions on page 28 for torch-firing)	8-12%
Art Clay® Silver-650/1200 Low firing clay, fires with sterling silver findings, glass, stones such as moonstone, garnet, and hematite	1472°F for 5 min. 1200°F for 30 min.	Kiln or torch (see instructions on page 28 for torch-firing)	8-9%
Art Clay® Gold 22K gold	1814°F for 60 min.	Kiln	15%

The firing times shown here are minimums. It will not harm the metal to fire for longer than is suggested. Doing so allows you to fire different types of clay together.

PMC® provides this chart to compare the varying strengths of standard PMC® with PMC+® and PMC3®. Notice that PMC+® and PMC3® do not require high firing temperatures for strength.

Strength After Firing

weak
pretty good
very good

PMC®

Firing Temperature									
° F	930	1020	1110	1200	1290	1380	1470	1560	1650
° C	500	550	600	650	700	750	800	850	900

Minutes										
5									
10									
20									
30									
60									▓
120									▓

PMC+®

Firing Temperature									
° F	930	1020	1110	1200	1290	1380	1470	1560	1650
° C	500	550	600	650	700	750	800	850	900

Minutes										
5								▒	▓
10							▒	▒	▓
20							▒	▒	▓
30						▒	▓	▒	
60					▒	▒	▓		
120				▒	▒	▒	▓		

PMC3®

Firing Temperature									
° F	930	1020	1110	1200	1290	1380	1470	1560	1650
° C	500	550	600	650	700	750	800	850	900

Minutes										
5		▒	▒	▒	▒	▒	▒	▒	▒
10		▒	▒	▓	▓	▓	▓	▒	▒
20	▒	▒	▒	▓	▓	▓	▓	▓	▓
30	▒	▒	▒	▓	▓	▓	▓	▓	▓
60	▒	▒	▒	▓	▓	▓	▓	▓	▓
120	▒	▒	▒	▓	▓	▓	▓	▓	▓

Finishing Fired Metal Clay

Silver metal clay comes out of the kiln or torch-firing with a powder-white surface color. Gold reflects a matte light yellow color. This is not a coating, but rather the silver particles themselves in an unburnished state. The white appearance of the piece is due to tiny silver particles sticking up like the bristles of a brush. Light reflects on the particles from different angles to appear white in color. As the particles are "flattened" or burnished, the surface will reflect the bright silver. The more the surface is refined, the brighter and shinier the silver will become. After firing, the finished metal pieces are pure silver (.999) or gold (22K–24K).

The same traditional tools and techniques that are used to finish silver and gold are applicable for finishing fired metal clay, except for a few modifications. Fired metal clay is more porous than regular silver and gold. Finished pieces will soak up patina or solder, and must be handled a bit differently to compensate for porosity.

Burnishing

Brass or Stainless Steel Brushing Scratch-brushing is the first step, and sometimes the last step, in finishing a metal clay piece. Brush the piece until the metal starts to shine. Brass brushes work very well for a satin finish. Jewelry suppliers and metal clay suppliers sell brushes for this purpose.

Brushing works well for finishing pieces with deeply textured surfaces. Some artists use small stainless steel brushes instead for a matte finish. You can brush the metal with gentle soap and running water to lubricate the brush, or brush the metal with a bit of baking soda and water to clean the piece. The soap or baking soda will also help if you are going to use a patina solution to reduce the amount of patina retained in the porous surface of silver metal.

Small scratch brushes are available for Dremel® or flexible shaft tools for small areas. Many of the projects in this book were finished with a brass brush alone. If you want a mirror shine, you will want to follow with fine sanding papers and burnishing tools.

Burnishing Tools Stainless steel burnishing tools are available at jewelry or metal clay suppliers. Burnishing adds sparkle and shine to the raised areas on the metal. This is usually the final step in finishing a piece. It's mentioned here because raised areas can be burnished immediately following scratch-brushing to

You can bring out the highlights of a textured piece by burnishing the raised surface areas. Go over the piece with a brass brush until the metal starts to shine. Alternatively, you can use a stainless steel brush for a matte finish.

By flattening the metal particles, a burnishing tool adds sparkle and shine to the raised areas of texture. This is usually the final step in finishing a piece.

A professional-grade jewelry or rock tumbler is used for burnishing fired metal clay.

complete a highly textured piece. Flat pieces can be progressively polished with papers first before using a burnishing tool as the final step. You can use other household items such as knitting needles, stainless steel kitchen spoons, or paper clips to burnish the metal, especially tight spots.

To burnish an item, hold the piece firmly and apply pressure while rubbing on the surface of the metal with the tool. The burnishing tool will compress the metal particles for a high shine.

Tumbling Another method for burnishing fired metal clay is to use a jewelry or rock tumbler. Choose professional grade, not a toy model. Mini-rotary tumblers are inexpensive and save a great deal of time if you plan on finishing a number of pieces. Prepare pieces by scratch-brushing beforehand. Fill the tumbler with stainless steel mixed shot. Mixed shot consists of rod, sphere, and disk shapes. This combination of shapes allows the shot to burnish the surface of the metal, reaching all of the nooks and crannies of the piece. Stainless steel shot costs more than steel shot, but it's worth it because it does not rust. Hollow pieces, such as beads, can first be strung on a wire to prevent shot from being trapped in the bead.

Follow the manufacturer's instructions for operating the tumbler. Tumble the pieces for about an hour. After 30 minutes, check the pieces periodically and remove them when they reach the desired shine and finish. Pieces begin to lose fine detail if they are tumbled for too long. Tumbling also work-hardens the metal for a stronger finished product. Jewelry supply catalogs and metal clay suppliers offer small tumblers, shot, and burnishing compound.

Filing and Sanding

Metal files Small, pointed files are used to finish rough or hard-to-reach places. Small jewelry files are available in sets from jewelry-making suppliers or model-making suppliers. File the metal in one direction. Follow with progressive sanding to remove the scratches left by the file. If you smooth and finish a metal clay piece before firing, this step may be unnecessary.

Nail files Fingernail files can be used on unfired clay. For fired metal clay, file the edges first with the file, followed by progressively finer sanding papers.

Sanding papers and pads 3M makes flexible sponge sanding pads, graded from medium to micro-fine, to finish both unfired and fired metal clay. The medium grit is rough and will scratch the fired metal; this grit should be used if you are trying to remove metal or sand a rough area. Move progressively from the coarse pads to the finer grits to remove scratches and finish the metal for a smooth finish. Follow with polishing papers if desired. Other types of wet or dry sandpaper from the hardware store can also be used to sand the finished metal.

3M Wet or Dry®Tri-M-Ite® Polishing Papers are thin flexible sheets for extra-fine polishing. These clothlike papers come in six different grits. You can cut the papers into small pieces that can be used to sand tight areas. You can create a mirror finish on metal clay, starting with the most abrasive paper and moving progressively to the finest.

Papers and Pads

3M Sponge Sanding Pads come in these grades:
Medium
Fine
Super-fine
Ultra-fine
Micro-fine

3M Polishing Papers are color coded, starting with green as the most abrasive and light green as the finest grit:
Green
Grey
Blue
Pink
Mint
Light green

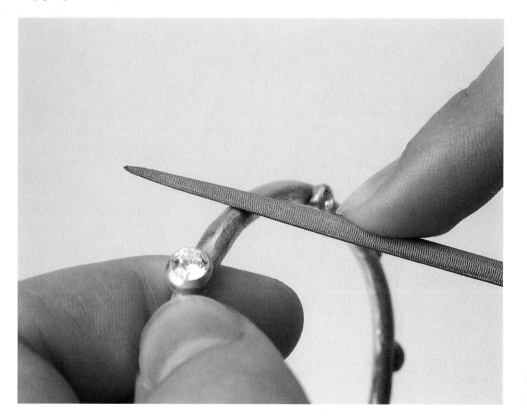

When using metal files, always file in one direction.

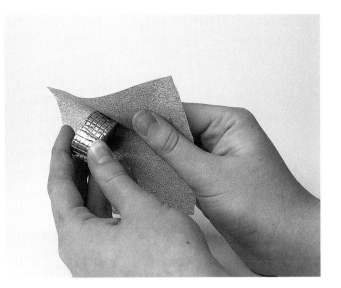

Create a mirror finish by starting with the most abrasive paper and moving progressively to the finest.

Buffing After you have sanded a piece with fine papers, you can buff it for more shine. Buffing pads and jewelry polish cloths can be used to polish the metal. Pieces can also be polished using a rotary machine or flexible shaft tool fitted with muslin buffing wheels and rouge to polish.

Soldering Metal clay is porous and can soak up solder, so be sure to follow a few important tips for success. The surface must be prepared first by burnishing or tumbling. This will compact the silver particles on the surface to make the silver less porous. Use one of the strong, dense types of metal clay, and make sure the piece is not underfired.

Care must be taken to remove the heat the moment the solder starts to flow. You may want to try soldering on a few scrap pieces before your final project. The nice thing about metal clay is you have the option of attaching findings, making loops, bails, and so forth, before the clay is fired, with no need to solder findings to the finished piece.

Patina on Metal Clay The same surface treatments that are traditionally used on sterling or fine silver can be applied to fired silver metal clay. This is true for changing the color or darkening the metal with patina solutions. There are solutions sold through jewelry suppliers that you can experiment with. Make sample chips of fired metal to keep a record of different patinas. Because fired metal clay is porous, it's best to brush the piece with baking soda followed by tumbling or burnishing, before soaking in a patina solution.

A common method to change the color or darken pieces is to use liver of sulfur, available at any jewelry-making supplier. It darkens by oxidizing the metal. Be sure to follow safety precautions. Work in a well-ventilated area with gloves to protect your skin. Liver of sulfur should be kept away from eating areas and disposed of after use. Check with local authorities on proper disposal methods in your area.

To begin the patina process, dissolve a few chips of dry liver of sulfur in hot water. Heat the silver pieces, running them under hot water first. Use a wire to dip the pieces into the solution. Dip the silver into the solution and watch as the color moves from golden yellow to blue and finally to black-blue. Remove from the solution when you like the color. Rinse the silver under cold water and polish with fine sanding papers and buffing cloths to remove the patina from the raised areas.

Use a wire to dip the piece into the patina solution.

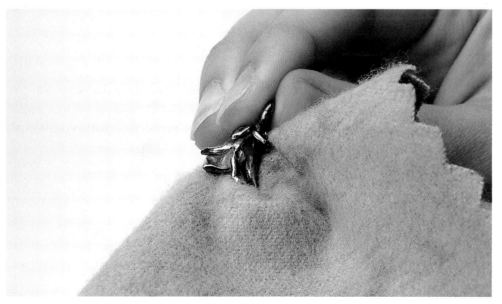

When your piece attains the desired color, rinse it under cold water, and polish it with fine sanding papers and buffing cloths to remove the patina from the raised areas.

Metal
Clay
Techniques

Textures

One of the best things about metal clay is that it is extremely easy to texture with stamps (metal or rubber) or with found objects. The clay picks up every detail of a texture, which is retained after firing to reveal a smaller version of the original that appears even more intricate. Textures can be found anywhere. Try fabrics, lace, netting, screen, silverware patterns, buttons, or other household items to press into the clay for great textures. Objects from nature such as leaves, seed pods, branches, and seashells make lovely organic textures on the clay.

Textures can be rolled or stamped into metal clay while the clay is still moist. A thin film of olive oil or balm keeps the texturing tools from sticking to the clay. If the clay is too wet, the texture might smudge. Wait just a few minutes for the moisture to evaporate, and try applying the texture again. If the clay dries out too much, the texture will be faint. Brush or mist the clay with water, and wait for a few minutes until the clay softens and try again. Unwanted marks can be wiped away while the clay is damp or lightly sanded off after the clay dries.

Textures add depth and interest to a metal clay object. After the metal clay piece has been fired and finished, you can enhance the surface to make the texture more obvious. You can bring out the highlights of a texture by burnishing the raised surface areas. Use a burnishing tool or agate to burnish the raised areas. The shiny burnished surface will contrast with the duller recessed areas. Another way to bring out a texture is to darken the recessed areas. Use a patina on the metal as directed on page 34. Buff the raised areas to bring back shine. These surface treatments will add depth and provide contrast to the surface of the textured clay for a rich look.

Creating Subtle Textures

Standard PMC® is a good choice for making charms because it shrinks more than the other clays, allowing for tiny details. Regular PMC® should be fired in a kiln for maximum strength. You can also make charms out of any other metal clay types following the manufacturer's instructions.

What you need to make this charm bracelet:

PMC®

Basic metal clay tools
(see pages 18–19)

Leather stamp tools
(The Leather Factory/
Tandy, see *Resources*)

Lace or screen for
texturing

Small cookie cutters or
Kemper Klay Kutters
(see *Resources*)

Purchased charm
bracelet

Jump rings

Flat back rhinestones
(optional)

Envirotex Lite®—2-part
epoxy (optional, see
Resources)

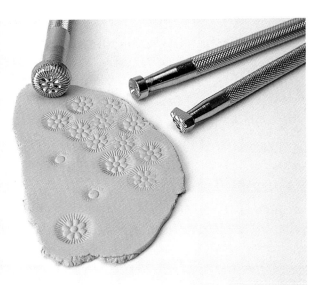

1 Roll out a sheet of silver clay between two strips of mat board about 1.5mm thick. Texture the clay with leather stamping tools, lace, or found objects.

2 Cut out shapes with small cutters to make charms. Use olive oil or balm to keep the cutters from sticking.

3 Layer smaller shapes onto larger ones to add dimension to some of the charms. Use water or thin slip to attach one shape onto another. Press lightly to adhere. You can attach other elements such as small balls or ropes of clay using slip if you want even more detail.

4 Poke holes with a needle tool or small drinking straw in the top of each charm. Let the charms dry on a flat surface.

5 After the charms are bone dry, smooth the edges with a nail file or sanding papers. Clean up the holes using a pin vise to drill the holes. Be sure the holes are large enough to allow jump rings through after firing.

6 Fire the charms flat on a kiln shelf (PMC®=1650°F for 2 hours). Finish the charms with a brass brush. Use polishing papers or a burnishing tool to highlight the raised areas for even more shine. Attach the charms to a purchased charm bracelet with jump rings.

For added flair, you have the option of gluing rhinestones onto finished charms with two-part epoxy.

Texturing with Stamps One great thing about texturing metal clay is the ability to make personalized objects, such as this I.D. bracelet. You can practice stamping a name or message on a scrap piece of polymer clay to gauge the spacing and placement of the letters before you start. Since a bracelet endures more wear than most pieces of jewelry, you will want to select clay that is one of the dense, strong types. Art Clay® Silver was used for this project both for its strength and low shrinkage rate.

What you need to make this stamped bracelet:

Art Clay® Silver

Basic metal clay tools (see pages 18–19)

Small alphabet stamps, rubber or metal (Alphabet stamps: Hero Arts set #LL435 and Alphabet & Number Set by The Leather Factory/ Tandy; see *Resources*)

Texturing tools (optional)

Drinking straw

Jump rings

Purchased chain and clasp

1 Roll out a sheet of silver clay between two strips of mat board about 1.5mm thick. Stamp the letters onto the clay. If you are using rubber stamps, you may need to use a bit of olive oil brushed onto the stamps to keep them from sticking to the clay.

2 Use a straw to punch a hole on each side of the letters, or you can punch two small holes on each side with a small juice box straw.

3 Use a blade to cut a shape around the letters and holes to make the I.D. plaque. Decorate the plaque with leather stamps around the border or leave plain.

4 Lift the decorated plaque onto a mug to dry. This will give it a nice curve shape for the bracelet. Use a nail file to smooth the edges after the plaque is bone dry.

5 Fire the plaque on a piece of fiber cloth (Art Clay® Silver=1600°F for 10 minutes). Finish the plaque by working with progressive sanding papers and polish to a desired finish. Blacken with patina solution to darken recessed areas (see page 34).

To finish the bracelet, add jump rings through the holes on each side of the plaque. Attach a bracelet chain and clasp fitting to the wrist.

Artists use rubber stamps, found objects, and simple tools to make wonderful textures on metal clay. Patina is added to enhance the texture after the pieces are fired.

Ancient Echoes Speak by Dawn Hale. A Mesopotamian cylinder seal was used to create the textures on this PMC® silver cuff bracelet, pendant, and ring. *Photo: Ralph Gabriner*

Egyptian Temple Painting Pendant by Eileen Loring. Textured using Uptown Rubber Stamps. *Photo: Dan Haab*

Jewelry tags by Sherri Haab. Made with jewelry tags, standard PMC textured with metal letter stamps, and 950 eyelets. It's a great project to do with leftover bits of clay. *Photo: Dan Haab*

Carved Metal Clay

Carving is a technique that involves working with dried metal clay for most of the project. It takes practice to carve consistently and evenly, but it is very satisfying. It provides an alternative way of working with metal clay for those who do not enjoy sculpting or other methods of working with wet clay. Carving metal clay is similar in technique to carving stamps, woodblocks, or linoleum.

Standard PMC® is the easiest clay to carve, and you can make detailed designs on the surface of the clay. Before carving, first make sure the clay is dried to a leather-hard stage. The clay needs to be set on a flat nonslip surface. A block of rubber-stamp material is an ideal work surface. A small pad of paper will work, too. This allows you to support and turn the flat piece of clay as you carve. Make sure you have the proper tools for carving. A V-shaped gouge used for carving wood or linoleum is used to make sharp outlines. There are several brands and sizes from which to choose. Dockyard Micro Carving Tools are a popular choice and are available at model-making, woodworking, or polymer clay suppliers.

As you begin to carve, make sure that your work area is clean and that other tools are out of the way. You will want to carve uninterrupted, without having to stop in the middle of a stroke. The best carving is deliberate, with the confidence to follow through each stroke. Make sure you follow safety measures and keep your fingers out of the way of your carving tools, as they are very sharp.

Carving on Dry Clay

Petroglyphs or "pictographs" were carved into rock thousands of years ago. They were carved to record events, communicate ideas, or to tell a story. Carving petroglyph images into silver clay produces striking graphic images that recreate the ancient look of rock art. The carved lines can be emphasized or altered in color by adding different patinas to the metal after the piece has been fired. Standard PMC® is the smoothest clay to carve, and it shrinks the most, allowing sharp detail in your carvings. You can copy existing images, or create your own artistic changes to personalize a piece.

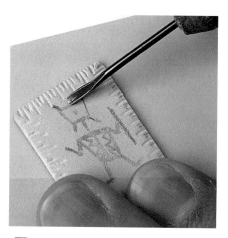

1 Roll out a sheet of silver clay between two strips of mat board about 1.5mm thick. Cut out a rough rectangle or oval shape about 1 inch in length to make a pendant. While the clay is wet, create a design around the border of the cutouts with a leather stamp. Or you can leave the shape plain. Let the pieces dry on a flat surface until the piece is leather-hard.

2 Use a pencil to draw a design directly on the surface the pendant. The unfired clay is fragile and could break if you press too hard with the pencil. If you make a mistake, you can use a soft eraser and start over. Another way to transfer an image is first to draw on paper using a soft pencil. Then, place the paper onto the dry clay surface face down and rub over it with a fingernail or blunt object.

3 Set the piece onto a nonslip working surface that can be turned as you carve, such as a rubber block used for carving rubber stamps. Use a small V-cutter to cut along lines with smooth continuous pressure, holding and turning the piece with your other hand as you carve. Move the piece as you make turns, not the cutting tool. If you make a mistake, you can fill cuts with fresh clay or smooth out small nicks with water.

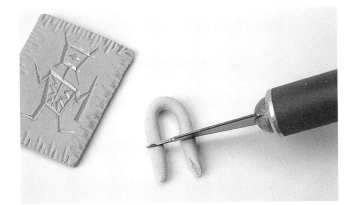

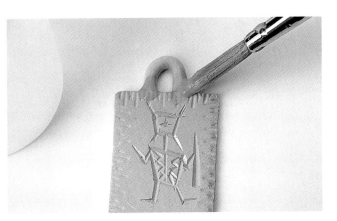

4 Roll a small snake of clay to form a bail for the top of the pendant. Cut the ends of the bail with a sharp knife.

5 Attach the clay bail with slip to the top of the pendant. Let the pieces dry until bone-dry and sand the edges of pieces smooth with a nail file.

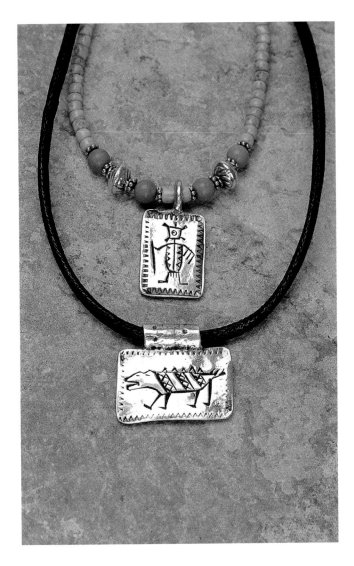

Choose one of these patterns for your petroglyph pendant.

Fire on a flat kiln shelf (standard PMC®=1650°F for 2 hours). Use a brass brush followed by sanding papers, working progressively to the finest grit for a smooth shine. Finish the pieces with a patina to darken the recessed areas (see page 34). Polish the raised areas with a buffing cloth to restore the shine. Hang the pendant from a leather cord or chain.

Carved Metal Clay Gallery

Rock art can inspire a collection of jewelry pieces. This series was inspired by different petroglyph designs from the four corners region of the western United States. To make the earrings and bracelet, follow steps in the Petroglyph pendant project. Hang the earrings from sterling silver ear wires. Use turquoise beads to make a bracelet, and attach a silver petroglyph charm with a jump ring.

Petroglyph bracelet and earrings, by Sherri Haab. These were made with standard PMC®. Patina was added with liver of sulfur. *Photo: Dan Haab*

Working with Molds

Making molds is addictive. Serious clay artists carry mold-making materials with them in their travels, just in case they stumble into interesting textures to cast, such as old doorknobs and other architectural details.

There are several materials available for mold-making, all with different properties. Rigid molds can be made out of polymer clay, and can be used over and over. Polymer clay is available in craft stores and can be molded and then cured, or hardened, in a conventional oven at 275°F. You can use scraps left over from another polymer clay project. Talc or cornstarch is needed to act as a release agent for the object. Use olive oil in the finished mold to prevent the metal clay from sticking.

Since polymer clay molds are rigid, you will want to avoid molding objects that will leave undercuts, or raised details, in the mold. They can get stuck in the mold. Super Sculpey™ made by Polyform Products makes excellent molds because it is soft to work with and very strong when baked at least 30 minutes. Bake all molds made with polymer clay for 30 minutes for maximum strength.

Flexible molds can be made with two-part silicone compounds. A flexible mold allows for undercuts. You can flex or bend the material to release the cast object. This type of mold cures at room temperature. There are several brands, including Belicone™, Mega-Sil™, and Silputty®, available at antique restoration or jewelry supply companies. The mixed compound sets up fast, so have the object you want to mold ready to use.

Another material used for mold-making is low-temperature thermoplastic. This material softens when you heat it and becomes rigid when cooled. It can be reheated in hot water and used over and over again. Protoplast™ is one brand name of this material. You can purchase the pellets by the pound (see *Resources*).

Making a Mold with Polymer Clay

Sometimes, you find a button that is one of a kind. You can replicate the button out of metal clay to make earrings, necklaces, or more buttons. An inexpensive plastic button from the fabric store will look antique when fashioned out of metal clay. Super Sculpey™, a polymer clay, works best for this project because it retains detail and makes a sturdy mold that can be used over and over again.

What you need to make a this antique button necklace:

PMC+® silver

Basic metal clay tools
(see pages 18–19)

Antique-style button

Polymer clay for the mold
(Super Sculpey™)

Cornstarch

Olive oil

14 fine silver eyelets or
wire (see *Resources*)

10 sterling silver jump
rings

Necklace chain

Toggle clasp

5 pearls

5 sterling silver head pins

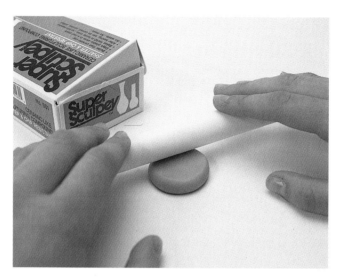

1 To make seven molded silver metal buttons, first roll out a thick pad of polymer clay. This needs to be deep enough to press the button into without hitting the bottom of the clay.

2 Brush talcum powder or cornstarch onto the clay and onto the button to keep them from sticking. Press the button into the unbaked polymer clay, and carefully remove it. You can trim excess clay away from the mold before baking. Bake the polymer clay mold on a glass baking dish at 275° F for 30 minutes. Let the mold cool.

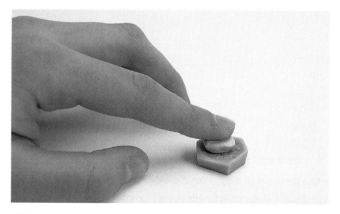

3 Coat the polymer clay mold with a little olive oil to keep the PMC® from sticking to it. Press a small ball of PMC® into the mold.

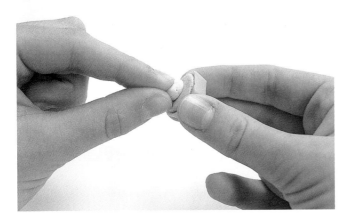

4 Carefully pull the clay out of the mold. A small piece of PMC® can be pressed onto the back of the molded piece to give you a temporary handle to pull the clay out of the mold.

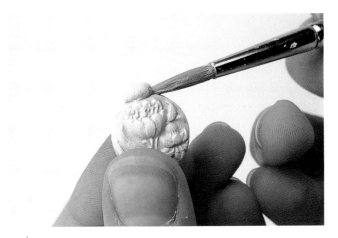

5 Let the buttons dry until they are firm enough to hold shape. Attach a ball of clay onto each end of each button with slip.

6 Insert a fine silver eyelet into the ball of clay on each end. Sterling wire becomes brittle when fired with the clay, so avoid using it in the unfired clay. Dry the molded buttons on a flat surface. Use a paintbrush with slip or water to reinforce the balls of clay. After the slip dries, use a small paintbrush with water to smooth out any imperfections. Let the buttons dry thoroughly.

7 Use a nail file to smooth the edges. Fire the buttons (PMC+®=1650°F for 10 minutes). Finish the buttons with a brass brush. Use polishing papers or a burnishing tool to highlight the raised areas. Blacken with patina solution (see page 34). Use a polishing cloth to buff the raised areas.

To finish the necklace, link the finished buttons together with jump rings, linking three buttons on each side of the necklace. Attach both sides to one central button in the middle, and add a chain and toggle clasp. Finally, add pearl accents to head pins.

To make the earrings, follow steps 1–4 for the necklace, then use a needle tool or sewing needle to make a hole through the molded button. Twist the tool down through the top and then back up through the bottom. (You can make the hole bigger after the piece dries with a small pin vise if you are worried about ruining the shape of the button while the clay is wet.) Follow step 7.

To finish, insert a sterling eye pin or silver wire through the hole of each button. Make a loop with round nose pliers for hanging. Attach a freshwater pearl with a head pin to the bottom of each loop. Hang the earrings from sterling earring hooks.

Two-Part Silicone Molds

Two-part silicone mold compounds are a quick way to make molds that are very easy to use. They set up quickly and are flexible. You can mold intricate pieces that will pop out easily because of its flexibility.

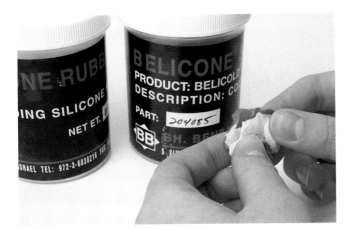

What you need to make molded shank buttons:
PMC®
Buttons
Basic metal clay tools
   (see pages 18–19)
Two-part silicone mold
   compound (Belicone™
   Silicone Rubbers)

1 Mix the two compounds included in the readymade silicone rubber mold-making kit. Mix the parts according to the manufacturer's instructions. For Belicone™ Silicone Rubbers, mix equal parts of each compound. Mix by kneading until the two colors are mixed.

2 Quickly press a button into a pad of the mixed mold compound. Let the button sit until the mold has set up.

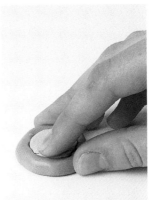

3 Remove the button from the mold.

4 Press PMC® metal clay into the mold, and let the clay dry in the mold. It will come out easily after it has dried.

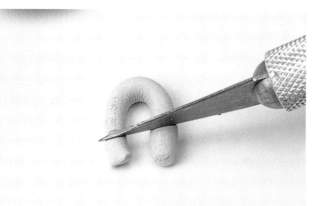

5 Roll a thin rope of metal clay to make the shank. Form the rope into a U shape and trim the ends to make them blunt. Let the shank dry.

6 Attach the metal clay shank to the back of the molded metal clay button with thick metal clay slip.

Fire the buttons on a piece of fiber cloth in the kiln (PMC®=1650ºF for 2 hours). Finish the buttons with a brass brush until desired shine is obtained.

Making a Two-Part Mold

Imagine turning something taken from nature into silver or gold. By making a two-part mold, you can replicate a three-dimensional object with metal clay. Both halves of the mold completely surround the object. The mold will pick up the details of bark on a twig to make an interesting texture for a bracelet. Polymer clay is used to make a strong two-part mold that fits together nicely to form a perfect replica of the branch.

What you need to make this branch bracelet:

PMC+®
Metal clay tools
  (see pages 18–19)
Bangle bracelet
  (for pattern)
Polymer clay (Super
  Sculpey™)
Talcum powder or
  cornstarch
Tape measure
Olive oil
Smooth branch or twig
  (without buds or protru-
  sions that will cause
  undercuts in the mold)
Cubic zirconia (optional)

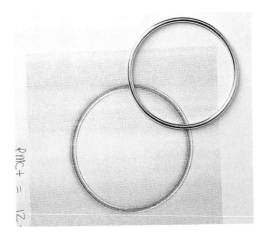

1 Copy a bangle bracelet on a black-and-white copier, enlarging the image 13 percent. This will be your pattern for the metal clay bracelet.

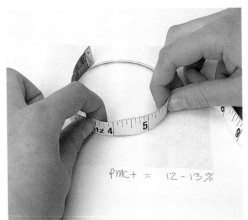

2 Measure the circumference of the enlarged bracelet image. A tape measure works well to wrap around the circle for ease in measuring. Use this measurement plus one inch to determine the length of the twig to mold. Cut a twig to the correct length.

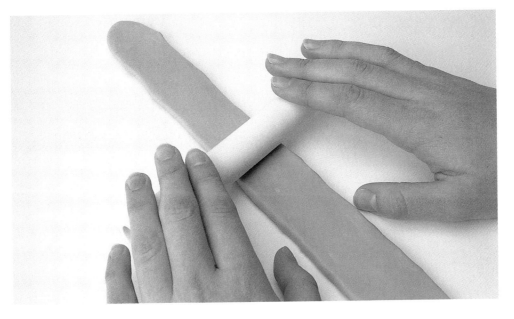

3 Condition the polymer clay by kneading it until soft and pliable. Roll the clay into a thick slab. Trim it into a long rectangle, an inch or two longer than the twig. Place the polymer clay slab onto a baking sheet before making the mold.

4 Brush talcum powder onto the entire surface of the polymer clay slab.

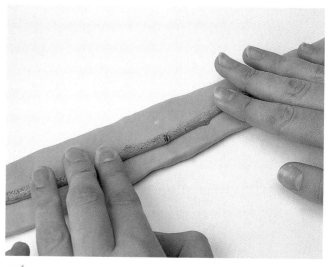

5 Press the twig into the clay until half of the twig is embedded into the clay.

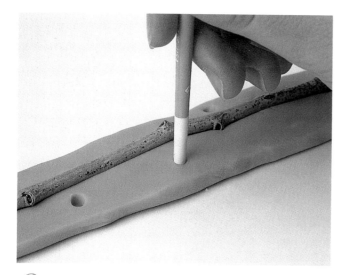

6 Make a few registration marks into the clay surrounding the twig. Carefully remove the twig and set it aside, remembering how it was set in the mold. Bake the polymer clay at 275ºF for 30 minutes. Remove from the oven and cool. Replace the twig into the baked mold.

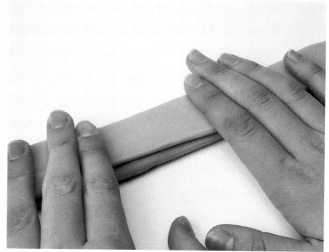

7 Roll out another thick slab of clay onto a baking sheet and brush with talcum powder. Turn the baked part, with twig in place, face down onto the unbaked polymer clay slab. Press firmly to ensure full contact with the twig and registration marks. Trim the sides of the raw clay to match the edges of the baked clay piece.

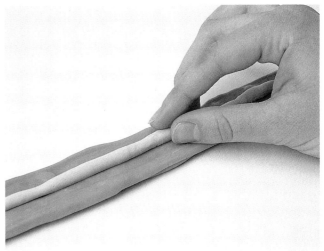

8 Place, unbaked-side down, on the baking sheet, removing the baked half and the twig. Bake at 275° for 30 minutes. Remove from the oven and cool. Both baked polymer clay pieces will fit together as a two-part mold. Brush both parts of the mold with olive oil.

9 Open a fresh package of PMC+® metal clay. Roll the clay into a long rope roughly the same size as the twig. Place the rope of metal clay into the bottom half of the mold.

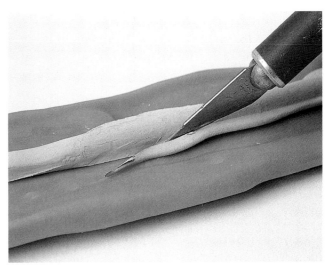

10 Place the top half of the mold into place matching the registration marks and press.

11 Remove the top of the mold and use an X-Acto® knife to trim the edges of the excess clay along the length of the metal clay. Replace the top mold and repeat the trimming process several times until the excess clay is almost gone and the seam is barely visible.

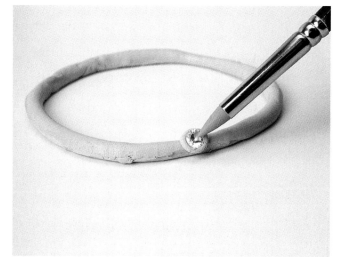

12 Remove the molded metal clay twig from the mold and place it on the copied pattern. Trim the ends off, and attach the clay with a butt joint. Blend the seam well with a clay shaper. Use slip and water to attach the joint. Let the metal twig clay bracelet dry.

13 When the bracelet is bone-dry, use a nail file or sanding papers to clean up the seams from the mold or any unwanted marks. Be careful, as the bracelet is still very fragile. At this stage, you can add small balls of clay with slip for the cubic zirconia. Press the cubic zirconia into the balls of clay just below the surface to allow for shrinkage.

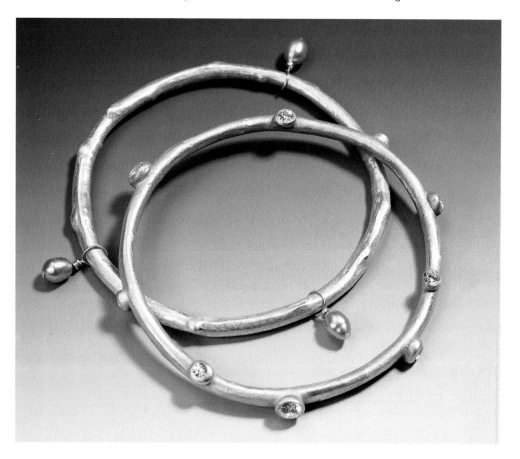

Fire the bracelet on a kiln shelf (PMC+®=1650°F for 10 minutes). Finish the bracelet with a brass brush and sanding papers.

Metal clay is so fine that it picks up incredible detail. Molded pieces look very close to the original model. Pieces are molded from ancient objects, antique buttons, and found treasures to make museum-quality jewelry.

Winged Victory by Dawn Hale. These are 24K gold PMC® intaglio relief earrings with 18K ear wires and sapphire briolette drops. *Photo: Ralph Gabriner*

Ancient Echo's by Dawn Hale. The 24K gold PMC® ring is made with an ancient intaglio relief; the 24K PMC® earrings from intaglios with sapphire briolettes and 18K ear wires; and the 24K intaglio relief pendant with embedded rubies on a 20K handmade chain. *Photo: Ralph Gabriner*

Celechée Earrings by Shahasp Valentine. Made from standard PMC®, pressed into three different molds making twelve components, which were assembled into the finished earrings, using white sapphires. *Photo: Hap Sakwa*

Grande Fleur de Lis Necklace #6 by Shahasp Valentine. Made from standard PMC®, pressed into 5 different molds, making 20 parts, which were assembled into the final piece, using lab-grown rubies. *Photo: Hap Sakwa*

Sculpting Metal Clay

Metal clay does not limit how you create a three-dimensional object out of silver or gold. Traditional methods require you to sculpt the original piece in wax, and then cast the piece out of metal. These are steps you can skip when working with metal clay. With metal clay, you sculpt the original piece and then fire it. There are several advantages: You can sculpt complex pieces without worrying about undercuts; you do not need fancy equipment; and your pieces will be one-of-a-kind. You also have the advantage of casting your finished pieces in metal if you wish to make multiples of your original.

As you begin to sculpt, think about the design of your piece. Detailed objects can be made in stages, combining small, simple shapes together to make up a complex piece. Keep the clay moist as you work, and use paper or other small objects to support the clay as you build. Most sculpting can be done with simple tools you may already have. The end of a small paintbrush, a round toothpick, or a clay shaper tool can be used to finish most sculpting projects. Small modeling tools used by the miniaturist are available in hobby shops or through mail order catalogs.

To fire a curved or round sculpted piece, support the piece in the kiln with fiber blanket or in Alumina Hydrate. For large pieces, you can save clay by making the piece hollow with cork clay inside. If a piece is heavy on top, you will want to fire it on its side or support it well so that the piece won't sag as it fires. You can also refire metal clay to add new clay elements or to make repairs.

Combining Simple Shapes

Simple shapes are used to sculpt a single rose for this pendant. Remember that the key to successful sculpting is to keep the clay moist as you work. Use plastic wrap to cover the clay as you assemble the rose. You can sculpt other kinds of flowers simply by changing the shape of the petals. The more petals you add, the more detailed the flowers appear. Look at petals found in nature for inspiration.

What you need to make this rose pendant:
PMC®
Basic metal clay tools
(see pages 18–19)
Cord for hanging (Round Lace by The Leather Factory/Tandy, see *Resources*)

1 Pinch off a small ball of PMC® metal clay, and flatten it between your fingers to make a small flat oval shape. Roll the oval into a coil to make the center of the rose.

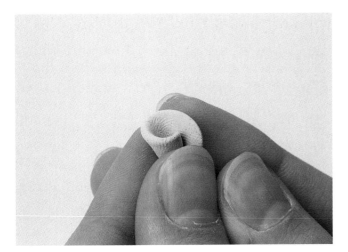

2 To make rose petals, roll pieces of metal clay into balls and then flatten them. Form each flattened ball into a wide teardrop shape. Start with smaller pieces and work larger as you add petals. Make 6–10 petals, depending on how big you want to make the rose.

3 Add the first petal with the pointed end up, pressing it to the center coil with water to adhere. Continue adding petals by attaching them one overlapping the last. Use water and a clay shaper tool to firmly attach the clay petals to each other. Keep adding petals until you like the size of the rose.

4 Use a blade to slice off the back of the rose to reduce the bulk and to flatten the back.

5 Let the rose dry while you make a loop. Roll a piece of metal clay to make a rope of clay. Bend the rope into a loop, and attach it with slip to the rose. You can add more slip as the piece dries for a secure bond and fix any flaws at this stage.

Fire the rose pendant on a kiln shelf (PMC®=1650°F for 2 hours). Use a brass brush to finish the rose after firing. Hang the pendant from a black cord to make a necklace.

Sculpting Miniatures These little garden charms look like they were created using the process of lost wax casting. Unless you are in the business of making production jewelry, this is quite an investment of time and money. The advantage of hand sculpting charms from metal clay is the ability to create intricate details that are not possible in cast pieces. You can make each charm straight from the clay, giving each a unique, hand-made quality. Standard PMC® was used on this project to make the tiny vegetables, fruits, and bugs. After firing, the charms are reduced by 25–30 percent, making them even more appealing. One lump of clay will make many miniature charms. Keep your unused metal clay covered as you work on each charm for this bracelet. The clay must be kept moist for ease in sculpting.

What you need to make this harvest bracelet:
PMC®
Basic metal clay tools
   (see pages 18–19)
Small flower and leaf-
   shaped cutters (Kemper
   Klay Kutters; see
   Resources)
950 silver eyelets
   (optional)
Silver jump rings
Purchased glass and
   stone bead bracelet

1 To make the pea, pinch off a small amount of clay and form three small balls. Flatten two long oval shapes to make the pea pod.

2 Place the oval shapes together, and pinch one side shut while leaving the other side open on your finger.

3 Place the three balls of clay into the pod using water to adhere. Press the sides of the pod to hold the peas in place.

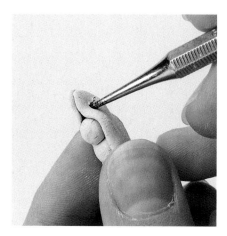

4 Poke a hole through the top of the pea pod with a needle tool. Let the pea pod dry.

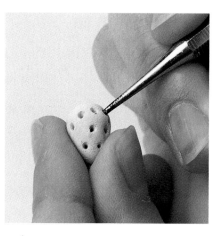

5 To make a strawberry, form a small ball of clay into a drop shape with the bottom tapered. Use a needle tool to texture the surface.

6 Use a flower pattern cutter or cut a star shape freehand from a thin piece of clay to make a leaf cap on the strawberry. Press the cap onto the top of the strawberry using slip or water to adhere.

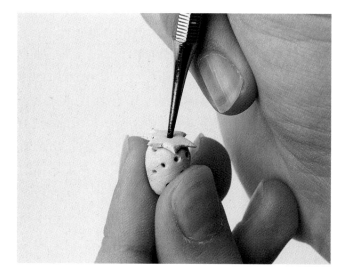

7 Use a needle tool to poke a hole down through the top of the strawberry. Bring the needle tool up through the bottom to meet the hole from the top so that a hole goes all the way through. Dry the strawberry.

8 For the ladybug, roll a small oval of clay for the body, and score a line down the center to make the wings.

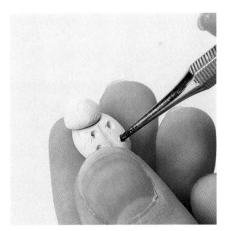

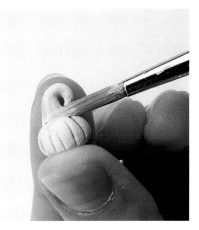

9 Add a small ball for the head with water or slip to adhere. Poke 2 or 3 holes on each side of the wings for spots on the ladybug.

10 Make a pumpkin starting with a flattened ball of clay. Score vertical lines around the sides with the back of a knife.

11 Make a stem out of clay. Pinch a long tapered piece of clay, making a wide base to attach to the top of the pumpkin with slip and water. Coil the stem over to make a loop. Work quickly with fresh clay to make the stem.

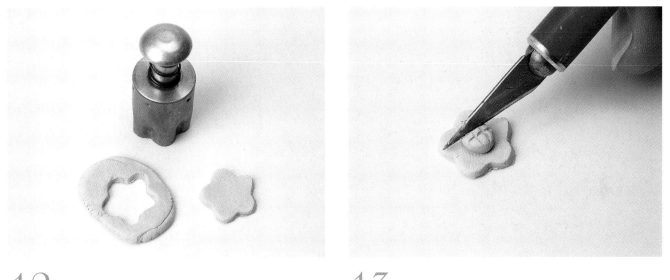

12 Next, use a pattern clay cutter to make a flower, or cut one freehand from a sheet of clay.

13 Press a small ball of clay into the center of the flower, using water to adhere. Press to ball to flatten. Use the back of a knife to score a crosshatch pattern in the center of the flower.

  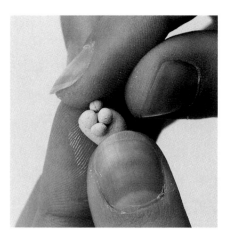

14 Pinch small pieces of clay into flattened teardrop shapes to make leaves. Score leaf veins with the back of a knife.

15 Use water or slip to attach the leaves to the back of the flower. Poke a hole through the top of the flower with a needle tool, and let the flower dry.

16 Follow the strawberry instructions in steps 5–7 to make the raspberry. Do not poke holes with the needle tool as directed for texturing the strawberry. Press tiny balls of clay to cover the raspberry, using water to adhere.

 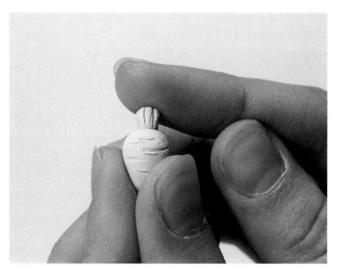

17 To make a beet, pinch a small piece of clay into a drop shape tapering at the bottom. Use the back of a knife to score horizontal lines to texture the sides of the beat. Use a pointed clay shaper tool to make a depression for the stem.

18 Make a stem with a small cylinder of clay. Make a texture of vertical lines with the back of a knife. Use slip to attach the stem to the depression on top of the beet. Add a fine silver eyelet into the top of the stem. Let the beet dry. The carrot is made the same way as the beet, only it is longer and thinner. Let the carrot dry.

Fire the pieces on a bed of fiber cloth
(PMC®=1650° F for 2 hours). Finish the
pieces with a brass brush. Add jump rings,
and hang pieces on a beaded bracelet.

Sculpted Metal Clay Gallery

The handmade look of sculpted metal clay adds to the charm of the finished pieces, separating the medium from traditional metal work. Sculpting is used in combination with other techniques to add detail and complexity to a piece.

Winged Heart Bead by Dan Barney. This is a hollow PMC bead with sculpted details. The bead was shaped over a cork clay form. *Photo: Dan Haab*

Shaman Bead #2 by Carl Stanley. Made with PMC® and glass enamel. This bead incorporates sculpted features to make the figure. *Photo: Brian Meek*

Beads

A bead core is needed to form and hold the shape of the bead while it is being fired. Cork clay, cold cereal shapes, and Creative Paperclay® are a few items that can be used to make bead cores. Drinking straws and twigs can be used for tube beads. You can coat the cores with wax if the surfaces are rough or sand them until they are smooth. Beads should always be fired in a kiln to avoid smoke from the core material and to make sure they are heated uniformly.

Cork clay, sold by metal clay suppliers, is an excellent material for making your own bead cores. This is because it will hold the shape of the bead and burn away during firing. It is easy to mold into any shape and dries to make a lightweight bead core. Dry the cork clay forms completely before firing.

Some materials are dangerous to fire because they emit toxic fumes. Cork clay is one of these; therefore, it should only be used on projects fired in a kiln, with the kiln door remaining shut during firing. Some of this smoke may escape from the kiln, so work in a well-ventilated area. Always fire beads made

Hollow beads made out of metal clay are easy to make. Each bead is hand-crafted with textures and details that are impossible to achieve with machine-made beads. They are very lightweight, making them perfect for designs that call for large beads.

with cork clay at 1472°F, as cork clay burns hot and may cause silver to melt if fired at higher temperatures. The clay can be applied directly to the surface of the cork clay while forming the beads. Unused cork clay needs to be stored in an airtight container to keep from drying out.

Creative Paperclay® is a material that is made with fine volcanic ash. It will not burn away during firing. This can be used when you want the bead to shrink as little as possible. The metal clay surrounding the bead will thin as it shrinks, so make sure you account for this. Make the holes large because you will need to chip the Paperclay® out with a needle tool after firing the bead.

Drinking straws work well for poking holes in beads, especially small, cocktail-sized straws. Needle tools can be used to poke smaller holes. Holes can be enlarged and cleaned up after the clay beads are bone-dry. For fancy beads, use texturing tools to decorate while the clay is still wet. Techniques and applications for other projects in this book can be applied to beads.

Cork clay is an excellent material for making the bead cores that support their shape during firing. But because of the toxic fumes it emits, *do not torch-fire beads made with cork clay.*

Creating Round Beads

Round beads can be used as part of a larger design or as a single element of design. Art Clay® Silver is a strong, all-purpose clay that works well for making round beads. You can also use other types of clay if you account for the firing temperature of the core material.

1 Make round cork clay cores. Let the cores dry. Roll out a thin sheet of clay (about 1mm thick or 3 playing cards thick). Cut a strip of clay long enough to wrap around the circumference of the bead and wide enough to cover the bead height.

What you need to make round beads:
Art Clay® Silver (Clay Type)
Basic metal clay tools
(see pages 18–19)
Cork clay (see *Resources*)
Drinking and small cocktail straws or needle tool
Texturing tools (Leather Stamp Tools by The Leather Factory/Tandy)

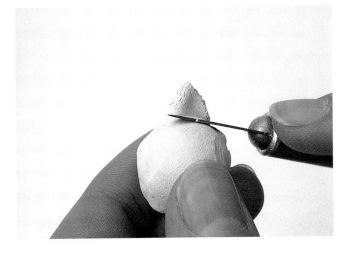

2 Cover the bead core with the clay, cutting away excess clay from the top and bottom with a knife. Use slip and water as needed to join the seams, smoothing the clay until the bead is completely covered.

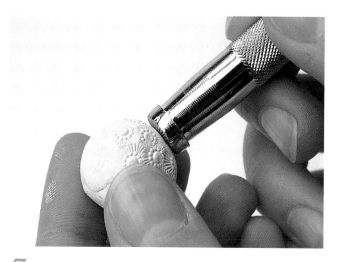 

3 Decorate the bead with leather stamping tools.

4 Use a small cocktail straw to make a hole on each end of the bead. Remember, the core burns away during firing, leaving a hollow bead.

Lay the beads on a bed of fiber blanket on a kiln shelf and fire (Art Clay® Silver=1472°F for 30 minutes). Finish the cooled beads with a brass brush, using a burnishing tool to highlight the raised areas.

Creating Tube Beads

Tube- or cylinder-shaped beads look great strung on fiber or leather cord. Readymade beads often have small holes that make it frustrating when you are looking for the perfect bead to fit over a cord. With metal clay, you can create tube beads around cores of any size to accommodate any project.

What you need to make tube beads:

Art Clay® Silver (Clay Type)

Basic metal clay tools (see pages 18–19)

Cork clay (see *Resources*)

Cocktail straws or needle tool

Texturing tools (Leather Stamp Tools by The Leather Factory/Tandy, *Resources*)

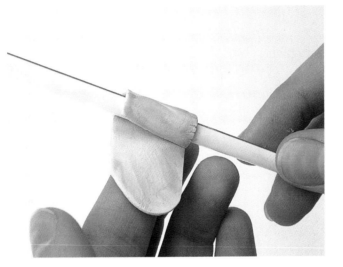

1 Roll out a thin sheet of clay (about 1mm thick). Use lace, screen, or silverware to texture the surface. Cut the textured clay into strips and wrap one strip around a drinking straw (textured side out).

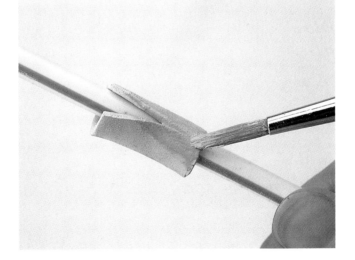

2 As you wrap the clay around the straw, you can leave a mark on the clay to indicate where it should be trimmed. Use water and thin slip to form a butt joint at the seams.

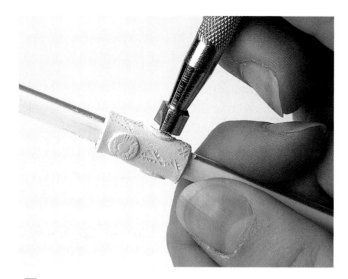

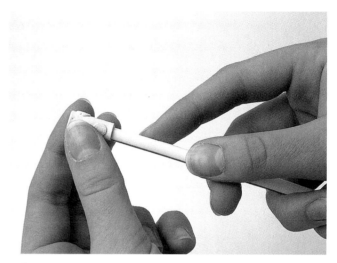

3 Add details to the beads by adding small balls of fresh clay. Attach the clay with water and thin slip. Press the balls of clay with a leather stamp to decorate. Let the beads dry until firm enough to hold their shape on the straw.

4 Remove the straws by gently twisting the beads off. Let the beads continue to dry until bone-dry. Sand the ends of the beads; sand in a circular motion on a piece of sanding paper or use a nail file to smooth the edges.

Lay the beads on a bed of fiber blanket on a kiln shelf. Fire the beads (Art Clay® Silver=1472°F for 30 minutes). Finish the cooled beads with a brass brush, using a burnishing tool to highlight the raised areas.

Creating Elaborate Beads

The artichoke bead looks very complex, but it's really just a combination of tiny overlapping pieces applied one after the other to complete the bead. Since it takes time to apply each little piece, Slow Dry clay is used to keep the bead from drying out as you work. This bead is worth the effort because it gets a lot of attention due to the visual and textural intricacy of the form.

1 Make a cork clay core in the shape of a teardrop. Let the cork clay dry. Roll out a sheet of metal clay about 1mm thick (3 playing cards thick). Cut out flat teardrop shapes with a teardrop-shaped cutter. Cut as many as you can fit out of the sheet of clay. Keep the clay covered with plastic wrap to keep it moist.

What you need to make artichoke beads:

Art Clay® Silver
(Slow Dry)
Basic metal clay tools
(see pages 18–19)
Teardrop shaped Klay
Kutter ³/₈" (Kemper
Tools, see *Resources*)
Cork clay (see *Resources*)
Chain for hanging

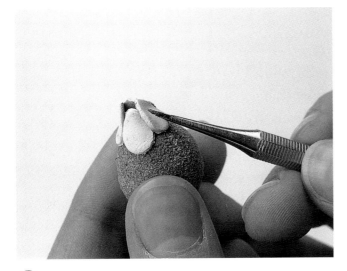

2 Start at the pointed end of the cork clay core. Apply the teardrop shapes next to one another, slightly overlapping with the pointed ends toward the point of the core form. Use water to attach the pieces. Make a vertical mark in the center of each teardrop shape with a needle tool.

3 Continue adding teardrop shapes in rows, each overlapping the last.

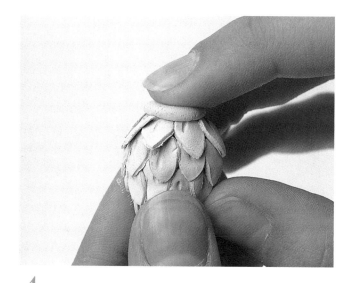

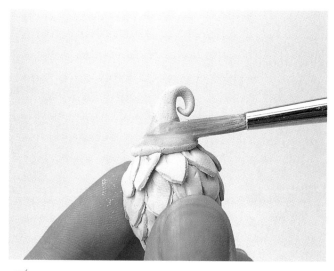

4 Finish covering the core with a round pad of clay on the top of the bead.

5 Make the stem of the bead with a tapered piece of fresh moist clay. Quickly coil the tapered end of the clay into a loop before the clay starts to dry. Attach the thick end of the stem piece with slip to the top of the bead. Decorate the pointed end with a small ball.

Fire the bead on a fiber blanket in the kiln (Art Clay® Silver/Slow Dry=472°F for 30 minutes). Finish the bead with a brass brush and hang it on a chain.

Beads embellished with gold, stones, and other metals stand as individual works of art. A single bead can be used as the central focus of a piece, or multiple beads can be used as elements of a larger design. Surface textures, along with sculpted elements, have been added to the beads shown here.

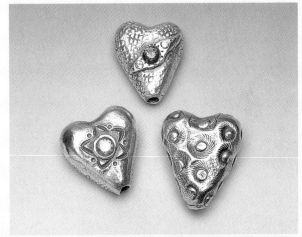

▼ Heart beads by Sherri Haab. Made with Art Clay® Silver and cubic zirconia. The beads were formed over cork clay and textured with leather stamping tools. *Photo: Dan Haab.*

▲ Beaded bracelet by Kate Ferrant Richbourg. Made with PMC+®, freshwater pearls, Ball silver, and a readymade clasp. The cubic zirconia was set with syringe clay. *Photo: Dan Haab*

▶ *Mended Heart* by Candice Wakumoto. Made with silver clay, 24K and 14K and aquamarine nuggets. *Photo: Larry Sanders*

Boxes and Vessels

Boxes and vessels are hollow forms and need to be fired with a core material just as beads do. A core maintains the shape of the box and prevents the piece from collapsing. Cork clay makes a sturdy armature to work on. It can be molded into any shape you desire and burns out during firing. For example, to make the first project in this section, the lidded box, you need to mold the cork clay into a cylinder shape. This is done by rolling the cork clay for the rounded sides, and flattening the top and bottom on a flat surface.

Let the cork clay dry overnight. Smaller pieces will dry faster, and using a dehydrator also speeds up drying time. You can sand the cork clay if you want a smoother finished piece. Create lids, handles, and other attachments after base pieces have dried to ensure proper placement and fit.

Fire cork clay projects in a kiln; do not use a torch, as the cork is combustible. Read the section on beads on pages 69–70 to learn about cork clay before beginning this project.

Constructing Functional Forms

Tiny boxes are not only charming, but functional, as well. Use them as a ring box or for a tiny gift. Use your creativity to personalize the box. A brass stamping of a bee was molded and then applied to the oval-shaped box in this project. The other boxes were embellished with hand-sculpted elements and textured with simple tools.

What you need to make this lidded box:

Art Clay® Silver (Clay Type) or other low-firing clay

Basic metal clay tools (see pages 18–19)

Cork clay (see *Resources*)

Texturing tools

Clay shaper tool (for smoothing seams)

1 Make a cylinder by rolling the cork clay for the rounded sides, and flattening the top and bottom on a flat surface. Then, roll out a thin sheet of Art Clay® Silver between two strips of mat board or 4 or 5 playing cards thick (1.5mm). Set the dried cork form onto the sheet, and cut around the bottom of the form to make the base. Press the silver base onto the bottom of the cork form until it sticks in place.

2 Before making the sides of the box, you may want to roll or stamp a texture into the clay sheet. After applying a texture, lay the sheet of clay texture side down before cutting. Lay the cork form on the clay sheet, and cut a strip of clay to match its height and long enough to wrap around the sides of the clay form.

3 Wrap the strip around the sides of the form to measure. Cut the ends cleanly with a blade to make a butt joint. Brush water on the seam and press until the seam is joined. Use more water or slip on the bottom of the box to join the seam of the base to the sides. A rubber shaper tool works better than your fingers for smoothing the seams if you have one. You can add more clay details to the sides of the box, using slip or water to attach.

Let the form dry, repairing any cracks with fresh silver clay and water. A clay shaper tool works great for working fresh clay into the cracks.

4 Make a lid by cutting a piece from a sheet of clay the same thickness as the sides and bottom of the box. Let it dry until it is leather-hard or dry enough to hold its shape. Add a thin rope of silver clay under the lid. Moisten the underside of the lid and the rope of clay with water. The circumference of the rope should be a little smaller than the opening of the box so that it will fit inside of the box after firing. Adjust the rope of clay if needed while it is still wet. Let the piece dry.

5 Turn the lid over, and add a ball of clay with slip to make a handle on top. Place the dried box and lid on a kiln shelf and fire (ArtClay® Silver=1472°F for 30 minutes). Finish the fired box and lid with a brass brush and polishing papers. Use a patina solution to darken recessed areas (see page 34). Buff the raised areas with a polishing cloth.

Place the dried box and lid on a kiln shelf and fire (Art Clay® Silver=1472° for 30 minutes). Finish the fired box and lid with a brass brush and polishing papers. Use a patina solution to darken recessed areas (see page 34). Buff the raised areas with a polishing cloth.

Forming Vessels

Metal clay is perfect for home décor or non-jewelry items. A vase made with metal clay will hold water and real flowers. Lavender was used in this tiny cone-shaped vase. Place dried flowers or a single rose in the vase for a different look.

1 Roll out a thin sheet of metal clay about 1mm (or 3 playing cards) thick. Oil the stamp with a coating of olive oil (olive oil in a spray form works best).

2 Press the stamp firmly onto the surface of the clay.

What you need to make this lace cone vase:

Art Clay® Silver (Clay Type)
Basic metal clay tools (see pages 18–19)
Large Rubber Stamp with a lace pattern (Victorian Lace Stamp by Stamping Up, see *Resources*)
Wire or ribbon
Piece of scrap paper

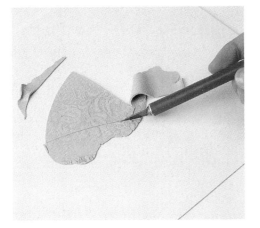

3 Use a knife to cut out the shape of the cone pattern.

Cone pattern for use in step 3.

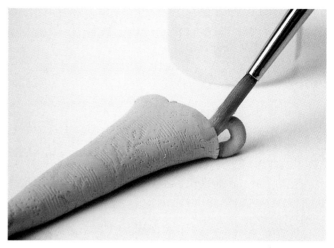

4 Wrap the clay around a rolled up piece of paper. The paper will support the piece as you work and keep the cone from collapsing as it dries. Smooth the seam on the backside with water and a brush. Blend the edges of the seam well, and make sure the bottom point of the cone is sealed.

5 Roll out a snake of clay to make a loop on each side for hanging. Attach them with water and slip. Let the cone dry. Once the cone is leather-hard, you can add more slip to strengthen the loop attachments. When the cone is bone-dry, remove the paper. Stuff a small piece of fiber cloth into the cone, and fire on a kiln shelf on a bed of fiber cloth (Art Clay® Silver=1600°F for 10 minutes).

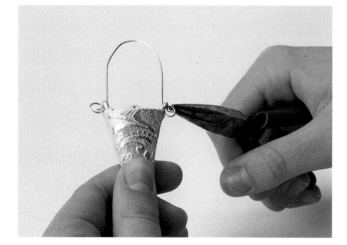

6 After the cone has cooled, use a brass brush to finish the piece. Hang the cone vase from a wire. Use pliers to bend the ends of the wire for a decorative finish.

Hanging the cone from a ribbon is a nice alternative to using the wire. Small flowers, such as lavender, work well for this tiny vase.

Box and Vessel Gallery

Boxes are fun because they not only look elegant, but are functional as well. They can be used as small trinket boxes or can be made into wearable objects. "Inros" are a popular style of Japanese medicine or trinket box that can be hung from a cord and worn as a necklace. Open vessels and boxes can be filled with decorative fibers, flowers, or other objects to add to the design of the piece.

Ipulani by Candice Wakumoto. Made with silver clay, 22K gold, 18K gold, blue topaz, amethyst, sterling silver, and Hawaiian coconut fiber. *Photo by Larry Sanders.*

Inro box pendant by Eileen Loring. Made with PMC®, polymer clay, a tassel and Buna cord. Eileen used a texture sheet to create the surface design. *Photo: Dan Haab*

Setting Stones

One unique feature about metal clay is the ability to set stones directly into the clay and then fire them in place, a quick alternative to the traditional method. Cubic zirconia and some synthetic (lab grown) stones, such as rubies and sapphires, are a few that will withstand high-firing temperatures. Rio Grande and several metal clay suppliers sell a variety of stones that can be fired successfully with metal clay. Make sure the stones you use are synthetic, not simulates, which can be made out of anything that resembles the stone (including glass) and may not be able to withstand heat.

Stones such as moonstone, hematite, garnets, and peridot can be fired with low-firing metal clays. Fire these stones at the lowest temperature possible and use either PMC3® (fired at 1110°F) or Art Clay® Silver 650 (fired at 1200°F). Soft stones—including turquoise, opals, and pearls—need to be added after firing.

Care should be taken when firing stones into gold because of its high-firing temperature and lengthy firing time. Cubic zirconia and corundums (rubies and sapphires) have been successfully fired into gold. The quality of the stone matters. You can set stones in projects combining gold and silver. Pre-fire the gold portion first, then add low-fire silver clay with stones.

Let fired stones cool slowly to prevent the stones from shattering or clouding. It helps to keep the kiln door shut to ensure gradual cooling.

To fire a stone in place, surround the stone with a bezel that will shrink around the stone. Make sure that the bezel is higher than the stone so that the stone does not "pop up" over the rim.

The following projects show different methods for setting stones, for both stones that can be set before firing and those that have to be set after firing. You can experiment and use whichever method you prefer.

Firing with Stones These pins were made using stones that can be fired in place. The stones were set easily into wet clay with a rope of clay providing a bezel for each. The Christmas tree and the butterfly pin were created using the same stone setting technique. Slight variations in technique and specific supplies for each are noted in the following instructions.

What you need to make these pins:

Art Clay® Silver

Art Clay® Silver
  (Syringe Type)

Basic metal clay tools
  (see pages 18–19)

Colored cubic zirconia
  of various colors and
  shapes

950 Silver pin-back
  (Art Clay® Silver)

**For the Christmas
  tree pin:**

Shade-Tex® Rubbing
  Plates (see *Resources*)

For the butterfly pin:

Brass stamping of
  Butterfly

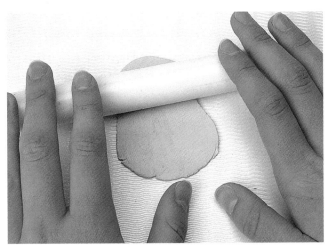

1 **To make the Christmas tree pin,** roll out a thick sheet of metal clay 2mm thick. Roll a texture onto the surface of the clay with a Shade-Tex® Rubbing Plate. Oil the sheet to prevent sticking.

2 Cut out a Christmas tree shape with a knife.

3 Press cubic zirconia stones onto the clay surface. Use the Syringe Type metal clay to surround each stone with a rope of clay. If the stone is large, make a second rope around each stone after the first rope has dried. Dry the pin until it is bone-dry. The bezels around the stones can be smoothed with water as the pin dries.

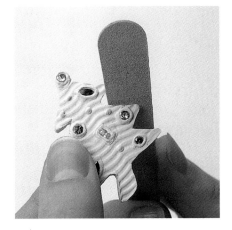

4 Sand the edges of the dried pin with a nail file until smooth.

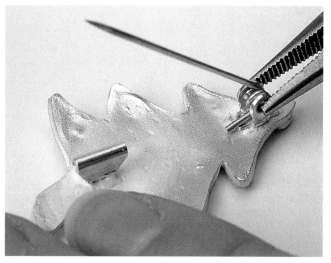

5 Measure the placement of the pin-back finding. Cut the pin portion of the brooch finding to the proper length if necessary, and file to a point. Use a thick slip to attach the catch and the hinge of the pin-back. Do not attach the stickpin part until after firing. Apply several layers of thick slip for a secure bond. Fire the pin on a kiln shelf (Art Clay® Silver=1472°F for 30 minutes). Finish the pin with a brass brush. Burnish the raised area of the texture with a burnishing tool.

6 Slide the stickpin into the hinge part of the finding. Pinch the hinge shut with pliers. You can buy a pin-back finding to glue on with epoxy as an alternative to the above method.

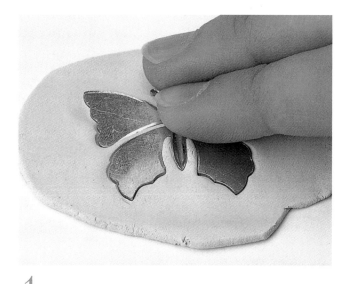

1 **To make the butterfly pin,** roll out a thick sheet of metal clay 2–3 mm thick. Press the brass stamping into the clay to transfer the texture.

2 Cut out the butterfly shape with a knife.

3 An alternative method is to make a mold of the stamping with a two-part silicone mold compound as directed on pages 53–54 (shank button project).

4 Follow the instructions in steps 3–6 for the Christmas tree pin to complete the project.

These pieces are reminiscent of vintage rhinestone pins that are popular collectibles today.

Making a Bezel for Stones

Semiprecious stones and metal clay are well suited for each other. Stones with inclusions, interesting textures, or shapes complement a hand-made metal clay bezel. This project uses a traditional bezel setting with a stone cabochon set after firing and finishing the setting.

What you need to make a bezel for unfired stones:

Art Clay® Silver (Clay Type)

Basic metal clay tools (see pages 18–19)

Leather stamp tool (The Leather Factory/Tandy, see *Resources*)

Clay cutter (optional)

.999 fine silver bezel wire, ³⁄₁₆″ x .013 (28 gauge)

Stone cabochon

Jump ring

Chain

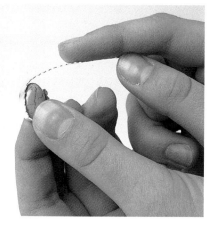

1 Wrap the bezel wire around the stone and cut the wire to fit, but not too snug. Make sure the cut is straight and neat. Roll out a thick slab of Art Clay® Silver about ³⁄₁₆″ thick—the same height as the bezel wire.

2 Push the bezel wire into clay only halfway deep. If you push the wire all the way, it will cut right through the clay, creating separate clay pieces after it shrinks in the firing process. To make an even border rim around the bezel, trim with a clay cutter or an X-Acto® knife.

3 Use paste or thick slip to fill in the joint where the ends of the bezel wire meet. Also apply paste or slip to reinforce where the clay meets the bezel both inside and out.

4 Texture the edge around the bezel with a leather-stamping tool.

5 Add a clay loop to the top of the pendant with slip. As the pendant dries, look for gaps around the bezel and fill with slip. Let the pendant dry until bone-dry. File the edges with a nail file until smooth. Fire on a kiln shelf in a kiln (Art Clay® Silver=1600ºF for 10 minutes), or torch-fire the pendant as directed on page 28.

6 Finish the silver with a brass brush and polishing papers. Place the stone into the bezel. Push the bezel around the stone with a burnishing tool.

To complete the necklace, attach a jump ring with pliers, and hang the pendant from a chain.

Setting Pearls Floral earrings made with PMC3® make a quick and easy gift. These drop earrings require very little clay, and everything is assembled prior to firing, with no need to solder. The earrings can be personalized for the recipient with a preference for a certain color. Pearls are available in a variety of colors, from rich purples and brown tones to light pastel shades of ivory, peach, and gray.

What you need to make these pearl floral earrings:

PMC3®
Basic metal clay tools
  (see pages 18–19)
³/₈″ and ¹/₄″ teardrop-
  shaped Kemper Klay
  Kutters
Fine silver wire
Epoxy
Two freshwater potato-
  shaped pearls
Two sterling ear wires

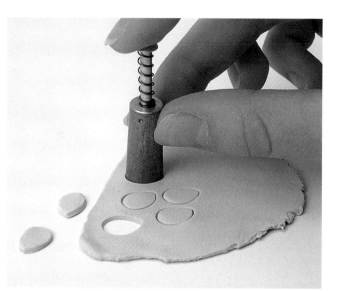

1 Roll out a thin sheet of metal clay about 3 playing cards thick. Cut out 5 ³/₈″ teardrop shapes to make the petals for each earring. Make one earring at a time so that the clay will not dry out. Keep the clay covered with plastic wrap to keep moist.

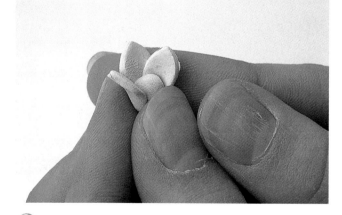

2 Make a small ball of clay for the center of the flower. Press the petals onto the clay center, overlapping one another. Use water to attach the petals to the center and to each other. Work quickly to keep the petals from drying out.

3 Cut out 5 small leaves with the ¹/₄″ teardrop cutter. Score veins on each leaf and attach the 5 leaves to the base of the flower. Overlap slightly and adhere with water. Add more water or slip to secure the petals and leaves.

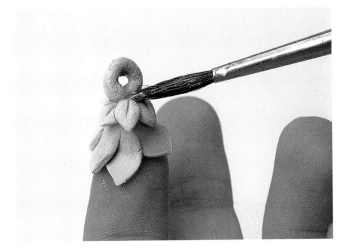

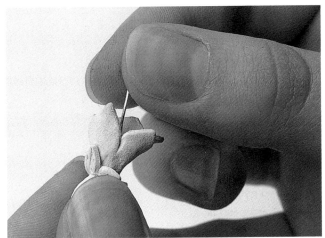

4 Roll a snake of clay and make a small loop to attach to the base of each flower earring. Use slip and water to attach, smoothing with a brush.

5 Turn each earring over, and insert a fine .999 silver wire into the center of each flower. Add slip around the wire to keep it in place. Let the flowers set until bone-dry. Fire the earrings on a bed of fiber blanket (PMC3®=1650°F for 5 minutes). Finish the earrings with a brass brush. After brushing, it's a good idea to tumble the earrings to work-harden the fine silver wires (see page 32). (Jewelry makers routinely work-harden metal by burnishing, hammering, pulling wire, or tumbling. In this case, the tumbler does the burnishing.)

6 Dip the finished earrings into a patina solution if desired (see page 34). Buff with a polishing cloth to remove the patina from the raised areas. Check the fit of the pearls, and clip the wires off if too long. Glue the pearls onto the wires in the center of each earring with two-part epoxy.

To complete the project, use pliers to attach a sterling silver ear wire to the loop of each earring.

Stones are set in a variety of ways. Many of the stones in these photos were simply pushed into the clay to set them and then fired into place. Other stones, such as pearls, are glued onto pieces after firing. Some artists use syringe-type clay to form clever bezels around each stone.

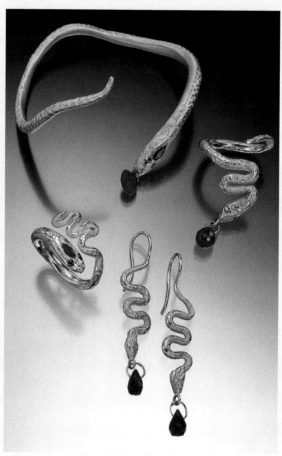

Heart of Stone Necklace by Melanie Bentley Shockley. This was hand-sculpted using PMC3®. A river stone from the Blue Ridge Mountains graces the center of the heart, embellished with white kishi and copper biwa pearls. Finally, it was handstrung with biwa copper pearls.
Photo: Bowyers Studio

Eden's Call by Dawn Hale. The snakes on these earrings are made of 24K gold PMC®, with embedded rubies atop freshwater pearls, and 18K ear wires.
Photo: Ralph Gabriner

Birthstone Star Charms by Sherri Haab. Made with Art Clay® Silver, with colored cubic zirconia. The pieces were cut with a small star cutter and the stones pushed into the clay. *Photo: Alyssa Dick*

Rings

Rings are great to make with metal clay for several reasons. One is that a very small amount of clay is needed to make a finished ring. The second is that the clay allows you a lot of artistic freedom in the design and shape of the ring. Making rings, however, requires more attention to forming and craftsmanship than other projects. You need to take into account shrinkage and strength in the design of your ring. This makes it tricky to size rings. Since the metal clay shrinks in the firing process and different clay types have different shrinkage rates, you must account for this to make a ring that fits properly.

The strength of a finished ring is dependent upon two factors: using the right clay and making a design that is structurally sound without thin or weak areas vulnerable to bending or breaking. PMC+®, PMC3®, or Art Clay® Silver/Slow Dry clays are good to use for making rings. Using Slow Dry clay prevents the ring from drying out and cracking as you form it around a ring mandrel (a tapered rod used by jewelers to shape and size rings). Having the right tools, such as a mandrel, is helpful in making a successful finished ring.

Creating a Simple Patterned Ring

Collect old silverware from secondhand or thrift stores to use as texturing tools on clay. Old butter knives provide a great collection of patterns that can be used to create relief textures on rings and other pieces of jewelry. Look for patterns with deep, detailed textures for best results.

What you need to make this silverware ring:

Art Clay® Silver (Slow Dry) or PMC+®

Basic metal clay tools (pages 18–19)

Mat board or playing cards

Teflon® paper (available at home product stores, used for cooking and ironing) or paper strip

Clear tape

Patterned silverware

Ring mandrel

Mallet

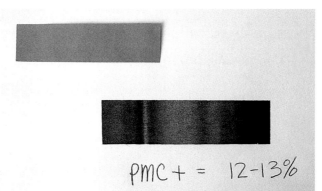

PMC+ = 12-13%

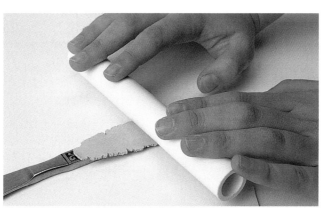

1 Measure your ring size with a strip of paper. Make sure that it fits over your knuckle. Enlarge the paper on a copier (12–13 percent for PMC+® or 10–12 percent for Slow Dry clay) to allow for shrinkage during firing. Use 1mm for a delicate ring and 2mm for a wider, thicker band. Cut this measurement out of paper, or a piece of Teflon® paper (which prevents sticking), wrap it around a ring mandrel, and secure with clear tape.

2 Roll out a small sheet of clay using mat board strips or 6 playing cards on each side, about 2mm thick. Keep a spray bottle handy to keep the clay moist and pliable. Spray the clay lightly. Oil the clay and silverware lightly. Roll the sheet of clay onto the silverware pattern to make a texture.

3 Trim the clay strip to the width you desire.

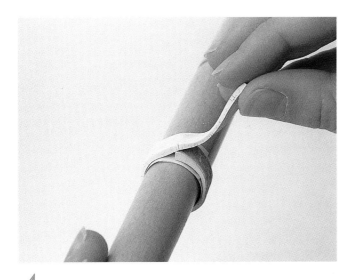

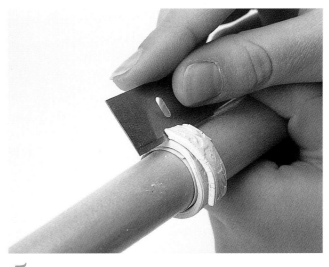

4 Wrap the clay around the mandrel until the strip overlaps.

5 Cut through the overlapped clay at an angle as shown. Remove the excess clay.

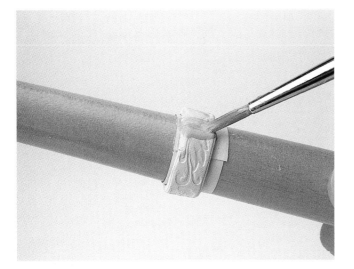

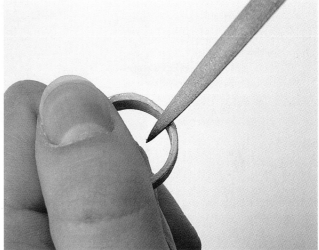

6 Moisten the cut edges with water and press to join. Do not worry if the seam is not perfect. You can fill in cracks or smooth out imperfections as the ring dries. After the ring is formed, let it dry on the mandrel until it holds its shape. Check the seam and apply more slip if needed. Remove the ring from the mandrel. Continue letting it dry on the paper. When it dries to leather-hard, carefully remove the paper from the inside the ring.

7 Smooth and sand the ring before firing. Bevel the inside edges with a small file, sanding carefully. Use water and a paintbrush to remove small imperfections. Fire the ring on a kiln shelf (Art Clay® Silver=1600°F for 10 minutes) or torch-fire the ring.

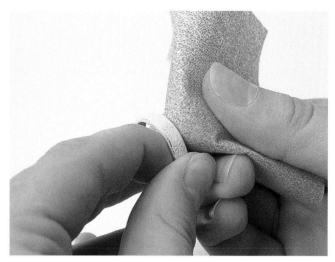

8 After the ring has cooled, you can shape it. If the ring needs to be resized or is misshapen, tap it on the mandrel with a rawhide or plastic mallet.

9 Finish the inside of the ring with sanding and polishing papers for a smooth finish. Brush the outside of the ring with a brass brush to preserve the delicate detail of the pattern.

Textured rings showcase patterns molded from heirloom silverware.

Making A Ring Bezel

Cut stones add sparkle to a ring. With the ability to fire stones into clay, you can take advantage of a variety of unique bezel or setting designs. The idea is simply to surround the stone with clay to hold it in place Be sure to choose stones that can be fired at high temperatures.

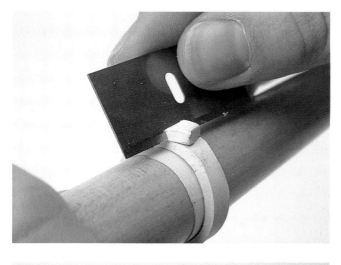

1 Make a band ring by following the instructions for the Silverware Ring on page 94 (steps 1–6). Omit the application of texture to the ring. Cut through the overlapped clay at an angle as shown. Remove the excess clay.

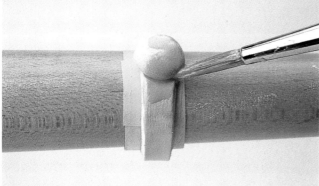

2 After you have joined the band at the seam, attach a ball of clay over the seam with slip and water.

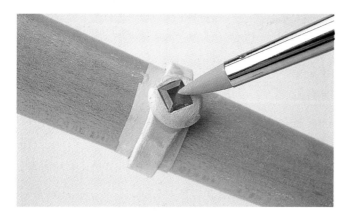

3 Push a cubic zirconia into the ball of clay until the stone is just below the surface. Add more slip at the connection and fix imperfections as the ring dries if needed. Let the ring set until bone-dry. Finish by following steps 7–9 in the Silverware Ring project. Remember to cool a ring containing a stone slowly. To be extra safe leave the kiln door shut until cool or air-cool if using a torch.

Birthstone rings are a fun project to make, and there are a variety of colorful lab-grown stones from which to choose .

Ring Gallery

Rings can be made with an individual's style in mind. Unusual shapes and textures add to the intrigue of each artist's interpretation of a design. Handmade rings that are less than perfect have a certain charm. They look like antiquities made by silversmiths before modern machinery made it possible to mass produce rings and other jewelry items.

Organic Ring #21 by Shahasp Valentine. From the "Organic Series" of naturally inspired forms. Made with fine silver PMC® with black pearl. *Photo: Hap Sakwa*

Buried Treasure Rings by Dawn Hale. Made with 24K gold PMC® with rubies, diamonds, and a diamond briolette (diamonds set after firing). *Photo: Ralph Gabriner*

Gold Metal Clay

Gold clay fires to a beautiful, rich yellow-gold color. Since it is pure gold, it is more expensive than silver metal clay. This high-karat gold is softer than 14K or 18K gold. Keep this in mind as you design and construct pieces to wear. It may not be appropriate for pieces that endure impact, such as ring shanks. The clay itself is very smooth and easy to work with. Water is used, as with silver clay, to keep it moist, attach pieces, or make gold slip.

Gold PMC® has the same shrinkage rate as standard PMC® (25–30 percent) and Art Clay® Gold shrinks 15 percent. This should be taken into account as you form pieces with gold. If you want to use gold to accent silver, there are several methods of combining gold and silver. One way to achieve this is to add a layer of gold with gold slip. To make gold slip, water is added to gold clay until it has the consistency of cream. Apply three even coats of slip to an unfired silver piece, drying well between coats. The unfired gold layer should have a uniform brown color. Fire the piece using a torch following the torch-firing instructions on page 28 as you would for silver.

Another way to combine gold and silver is by simply forming pieces using a combination of gold and silver clay. Since gold clay fires at a higher temperature (1830°F for 2 hours) than silver, you will want to make the gold portion of a project first, and then fire the combined gold/silver clay part with a second firing at the lower temperature required by the silver clay.

Combining Gold and Silver

Designs derived from nature date back to the earliest examples of gold jewelry created by artisans of ancient civilizations. Gold clay has a wonderful texture that lends itself to replicating the jewelry of ages past. Petals can be shaped, folded, and creased easily to form delicate flowers and botanical shapes. The finished pieces glow with the rich color characteristic of high-karat gold.

What you need to make these gold floral pendant and earrings:

PMC® Gold

PMC+® Silver

Basic metal clay tools (see pages 18–19)

Small heart Klay Kutters 5/16″ and 7/16″ (Kemper tools, see *Resources*)

Cubic zirconia

Gold jump rings

Gold chain

Gold ear wires

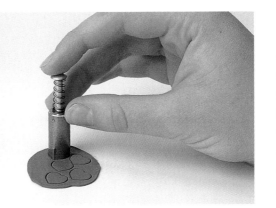

1 Roll out a thin sheet of gold metal clay (about 3 playing cards thick). For the pendant, cut 5 hearts out of the clay with the 7/16″ heart pattern cutter. Cut out 5 smaller hearts with the 5/16″ heart pattern cutter for each earring.

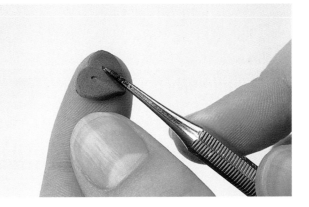

2 Use a needle tool to make two grooves in a V shape on each heart to make flower petals.

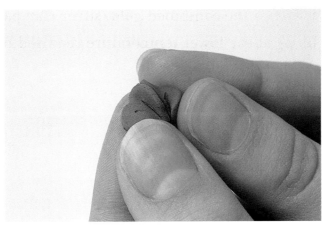

3 Attach the heart petals next to one another in a cluster of 5 petals for the pendant and 5 petals for each earring. Apply water to help join the petals.

4 Use a clay shaper or a paintbrush to blend the points of the petals together in the center of each flower. Roll gold metal clay into a long skinny rope, and cut off small sections, approximately ½″ long, to make a loop for each flower. Join the ends with water and a clay shaper or brush to join.

5 Attach gold metal clay loops to the top and back of each flower with water, pressing with a clay shaper tool to attach the loops. Fire the flower pendant and the earrings on a flat kiln shelf in a kiln (PMC® Gold=1830°F for 2 hours). After the finished pieces are cool, brush the flowers with a brass brush to burnish the gold.

6 Roll a small ball of silver clay and press into the center of each flower, using PMC+® slip to attach. Press a cubic zirconia into the ball of clay until the stone is just below the surface. Texture the edges of the silver clay around the stone with a needle tool for decoration.

7 Fire the flower pieces again (PMC+®=1650°F for 10 minutes). Finish the earrings with a brass brush. Sand the edges with polishing papers until smooth.

To complete the project, hang the pendant from a gold chain
and the earrings from gold ear wires.

Gold Metal Clay Gallery

Pieces can be sculpted out of solid gold clay, or several coats of gold clay "slip" can be applied to the surface of silver to accent a piece.

▼ *Wave Necklace #14* by Shahasp Valentine. Hand-formed fine silver and 24K gold PMC® with freshwater pearls and a white sapphire. *Photo: Shahasp Valentine*

▶ Pin by Chris Darway. Made with PMC+® on mesh, 950 wire, 14K gold, and 24K gold Keum-boo (the Korean technique used to apply 24K gold to silver). *Photo: Chet Bolins*

▲ *Freshwater Pearl Buds* by Dawn Hale. The "leaves," made with 24K gold PMC®, hold the freshwater pearl "buds" on these earrings and necklace. *Photo: Ralph Gabriner*

Silver Metal Paper

Silver metal clay is available in flexible, paper-thin sheets. They were formulated to drape and fold like fabric or to be cut or punched like paper. It is very flexible and does not dry out while you are working with it. If you prefer to use Art Clay® Silver brand, make sure you ask for Paper Type, as they also produce a Sheet Type with different properties. The Sheet Type is a pre-rolled sheet of metal clay, which is thicker than paper and can dry out. PMC® calls their paper "Sheet," which differs from the Sheet Type by Art Clay® Silver, so it's easy to get confused. Paper-type clay can be used by itself or in combination with other metal clay products.

There are several popular techniques for this type of clay. It can be cut into thin strips and woven or braided. Like fabric, it can be folded, pleated, or draped loosely over a base piece. For applications related to paper crafts, it can be folded into origami shapes for a finished product that is made of pure silver paper. Craft and scrapbook stores sell a variety of paper punches in many different designs. These work very well on the paper type of clay. Novelty scissors with different cutting edges are also very useful and are available at craft stores.

Use water or thinned white glue to adhere pieces of paper clay together or to a base piece of silver clay. If you want thicker sheets, several sheets of paper clay can be laminated or layered. To layer sheets, spray or brush water on the surface of a sheet of paper clay. Lay another piece on top and press the layers together. Wait for a few minutes for the layers to laminate before cutting or shaping.

Care must be taken when torch-firing thin sheets of silver clay. Overheating can cause thin areas to melt quickly on the surface. You will want to watch closely when firing paper-type clay, or use a kiln to fire.

Creating Patterns with Paper Punches

The casual style of these simple pendants makes them a great gift for a recipient of any age. With the popularity of paper crafts, there are numerous paper punches on the market from which to choose. Make seasonal pendants using holiday punches and colored crystal beads to accent.

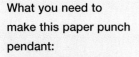

What you need to make this paper punch pendant:

PMC® Sheet

PMC+® Silver Metal Clay

Basic metal clay tools
  (see pages 18–19)

Shade-Tex® Rubbing
  Plates (see *Resources*)

Small novelty paper
  punches

³/₄″ square pattern cutter

White glue (Sobo® or
  Elmer's®)

Sterling silver jump rings

Sterling silver eye pins
  and head pins

Glass beads

Purchased sterling
  silver chain

1 Punch out small shapes from the PMC® Sheet using paper punches. Keep in mind that you can use the positive or the negative space from the punched designs. Set the punched shapes aside. Roll out a thick sheet of PMC+® about 3mm thick, or thicker if you want a double-sided pendant. Texture the clay with the rubbing plates or use other textures on the surface of the clay. Cut out small square shapes with a cutter or by hand.

2 Apply white glue to the punched pieces with a clay shaper or small brush and press onto the prepared clay squares.

3 Use a needle tool to poke a hole at the top and one at the bottom of the pendant.

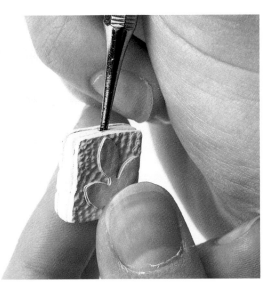

4 If you made a thick two-sided pendant, poke a hole can vertically down through the pendant with a needle tool. Poke the needle tool halfway through starting at the top, then up through the bottom to complete the hole.

5 Add a small amount of water with a brush around the edges of the punched designs to make sure the punched shape is well attached to the square pendant base. Dry the pendants on a flat surface. Sand the edges lightly with a nail file.

Fire the pendants on a kiln shelf (PMC+®=1650°F for 10 minutes). Finish the pendants with a brass brush and polishing cloths. Attach jump rings through the top hole for hanging. String glass beads onto eye and head pins. Attach the beaded wires to the bottom of the pendant using pliers to make a loop.

Shaping Metal Paper

This perfume vial kit was originally designed to be used for a wood-turning project. The brass tube is the part that is meant to be covered with wood. Brass can be fired with metal clay, making this kit perfect for metal clay projects. The brass serves as a base or armature on which to add a layer of metal clay. It also adds strength to the piece. Use the finished vial for a necklace or a keychain.

What you need to make this paper punch perfume vial:

PMC® Sheet

PMC+® Silver Metal Clay

Basic metal clay tools
 (see pages 18–19)

Leaf paper punch

Shade-Tex® Rubbing
 Plates (see *Resources*)

White glue (Sobo®,
 Elmer's®)

Brass perfume vial kit
 (Woodworker's Supply,
 see *Resources*)

Cord for hanging

1 Roll out a thin sheet of PMC+® clay about 1mm (or 3 playing cards) thick. Texture the sheet with a rubbing plate or other texturing material. Cut a rectangle of clay 2mm longer than the height of the brass tubing for the perfume vial. Center the tube from top to bottom with about 1mm extra metal clay on each end.

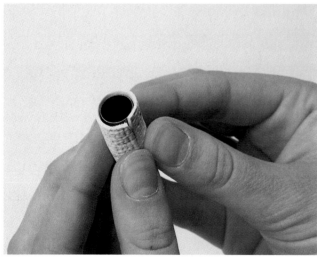

2 Wrap the metal clay around the brass tube loosely, leaving about a 1mm gap all the way around to allow for shrinkage. Apply slip to the seam, and press the seam to join. Use a clay shaper to blend the seam.

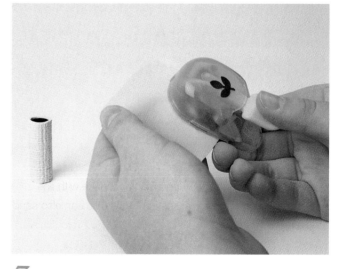

3 Punch out shapes from the PMC® Sheet with a leaf paper punch. Punch the leaves out in a row, and save both the positive (leaf cutouts) and the negative background strip of clay. Cut the background strip to fit around the clay-covered tube.

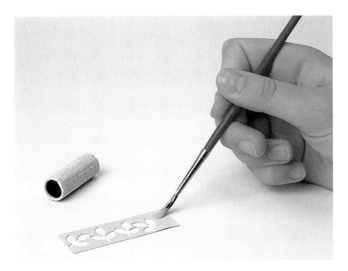

4 Apply water or white glue to the background strip of clay with a brush. Wrap the strip around the tube.

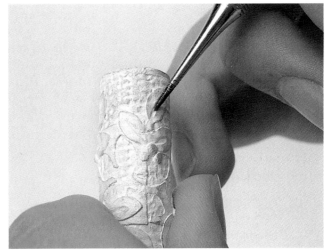

5 Attach the leaf shapes on the tube, layering the leaves over the background strip. Use a needle tool to score veins in the leaves. Use water on a brush to fix any unattached edges. Let the tube set until bone-dry.

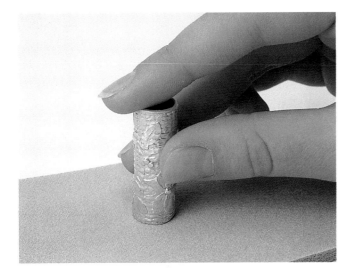

6 Sand the ends of the tube on a flat surface with fine sandpaper. Sand in a circular motion lightly. You can also sand after firing if the clay tube is thin and fragile. Fire the tube on a bed of fiber blanket (PMC+®=1650°F for 10 minutes). If you have any splitting at the seam after firing, you can use more metal clay and slip to repair the seam and refire. Finish the tube with a brass brush and patina if desired.

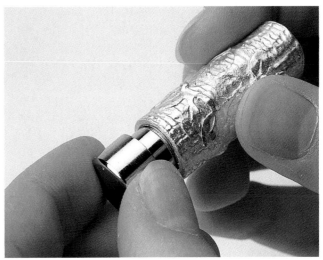

7 Attach the bottom and top pieces from the perfume vial kit.

To complete the necklace, attach the perfume vial to a cord.

Making Beads from Scraps

This is a project to use up all of the little scraps of PMC® Sheet left over from other projects. It's also really quick and fun to do. The chopped pieces of sheet make a great texture on the clay that is hard to achieve in other ways.

What you need to make these chopped PMC® Sheet beads:

Left over scraps of PMC® Sheet

PMC+® Silver Metal Clay

Basic metal clay tools (see pp. 18–19)

Dried cork clay forms (see instructions on pages 69–70 to make cork forms for beads)

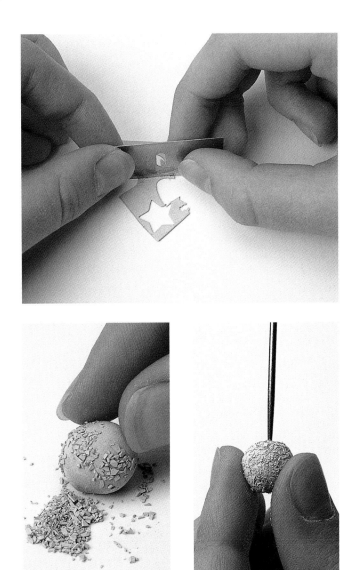

1 Chop the PMC® Sheet scraps left over from other projects on a flat work surface with a small blade until the scraps look like chopped breadcrumbs.

2 To make round beads, follow the instructions on page 71 for covering a cork form. Roll the clay beads in the chopped PMC® scraps while the clay is still moist. (See photo on far left.)

3 Pierce the top and bottom of the beads to make a hole for stringing.

Fire the beads on a fiber blanket on a kiln shelf in a kiln (1472°F for 30 minutes; remember cork clay needs to be fired at a lower temperature). Finish the beads with a brass brush. Burnish the surface with a burnishing tool for a diamond sparkle finish. String the silver beads with glass beads to make bracelets or necklaces.

Thin sheets of metal clay are useful to provide texture to the pieces shown here. Layers of PMC® sheet are folded and applied to a base piece for an interesting effect on a cuff bracelet. A small heart paper punch was used to create tiny details for the picture frame pendant.

Cuff bracelet by Kate Ferrant Richbourg. Made with fine silver PMC+®, PMC® Sheet, and lab-grown sapphires.
Photo: Dan Haab

Sisters by Sherri Haab. Made with fine silver PMC+®, PMC® Sheet, photo, and epoxy resin. *Photo: Dan Haab*

Epoxy Resin

Epoxy resin is a quick and easy alternative to using traditional glass enameling on metal. Epoxy resin is easy to use, inexpensive, and readily available in craft or hardware stores. Envirotex Lite®, Colores™, and Devcon 2-Ton® Clear Epoxy are some brand names. Some brands are clear, and some add color to the resin. There is a wide range of techniques you can experiment with to achieve interesting effects.

Dry pigment color can be added to the clear resin. Add a little to create translucent color and more for an opaque mixture. Other materials can be layered or mixed in, such as glitter, sand, gold or silver leaf, paper, photographs, or rhinestones. Liquids such as oil paints may react with the resin, so it is best to stick with dry materials.

Epoxy resin is sold in a two-part mixture. Resin and a hardener are mixed together thoroughly and then applied to the form. The resin will cure at room temperature, curing faster in a warm area. The proportions for mixing vary from brand to brand. Follow the manufacturer's instructions carefully for success. Experiment with the mixture that comes in two equal parts, which is easily obtainable from the hardware store. Dry pigment can be added to this resin, or it can be left clear if used over photos or paper.

Using Clear Epoxy Resin

Using Clear Epoxy Resin Tiny pictures set in handmade silver frames are a way to preserve memories. Clear resin protects the images and looks like glass in the frames. Reduce photos by scanning, or use a good color copier to reduce old photos and images for the frames. The finished framed images make great charm bracelets and necklaces for Mother's Day, birthdays, baby showers, or wedding gifts.

What you need to make this picture frame:
PMC®
Basic metal clay tools (see pages 18–19)
Small cookie cutters or Kemper Klay Kutters (smaller cutter for the inside of the frame and a larger one for the outside; see *Resources*)
Images reduced on a copier
Mod Podge® decoupage glue
Paintbrush for glue
Envirotex Lite® two-part epoxy resin
Toothpicks or old paintbrush

1 Roll out a thin sheet of PMC® about 2–3 playing cards thick. Cut the PMC® sheet in half to make a sheet for the base and one for the frame. Texture the frame sheet, and cut out the inside shape of the frame from the textured clay with a small clay cutter.

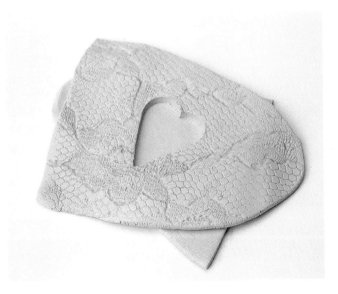

2 Brush water between the two sheets of clay and place the cut textured sheet on top of the base sheet of clay. Press the layers to adhere.

3 Use the larger clay cutter to cut out the frame through both layers of clay. Use olive oil to prevent the cutter from sticking. Check to make sure the cut is even all the way around the frame. Remove the excess clay.

4 Use a needle tool to make a hole in the top of the frame. If you do not have room to make a hole, you can use fine silver eyelets or make clay loops instead. Let the frame set on a flat surface until bone-dry. Sand the edges of the frame with a nail file until smooth. Fire the frame on a kiln shelf in a kiln (PMC®=1650°F for 2 hours). Finish the frames with a brass brush and burnishing tool to bring out shine on raised areas. Patina the frames if desired before gluing images in place.

5 Reduce pictures or images on a copier or printer. Seal both sides of the pictures with a coating of decoupage glue using a paintbrush. Let the glue dry.

6 Cut the pictures to fit inside the frames. A few hints: If you press a scrap piece of paper into the finished frame, you can see where the paper conforms to the edges of the frame. The paper can then be cut to use as a pattern.

7 Mix the two-part resin according to the manufacturer's instructions, and use the resin to glue the image into the frame. Use a toothpick or an old brush to add a layer of resin to coat the surface. Let the piece dry (preferably in a warm room to speed drying). Refer to the manufacturer's instructions for more details on curing epoxy resin.

8 Add a jump ring after the frame has dried.

To make a necklace, hang the frames from a chain. You can also attach multiple frames to make charm bracelets.

Coloring Epoxy Resin

Epoxy resin enamel is used to simulate glass enamel in this project. Pigment powders are added to the resin for color and opacity. Epoxy can be mixed just like paint to create any hue. Choose three primary colors to start with, mixing a range of colors from those for a pleasing palette. If you make a mistake, simply remove the resin from the surface with a cotton swab or cloth and apply again.

What you need to make this epoxy resin enamel tie clip:

PMC®

Basic metal clay tools (see pages 18–19)

Rubber Stamp Block (Speedy Stamp™ Block-Speedball® Art Products)

Speedball® #2 V-shaped medium line cutter

Epoxy resin enamel (Envirotex Lite®)

Pigment powders (Jacquard® Pearl Ex Powders in several colors; see *Resources*)

Toothpicks

Purchased tie clip finding

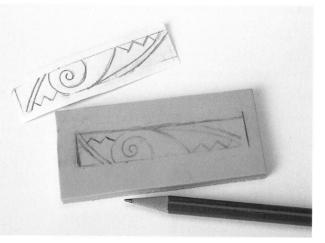

1 Draw a geometric design with paper and pencil that is ¹/₂″ wide by 2³/₄″ long. Rub the image face down on the rubber stamp block to transfer.

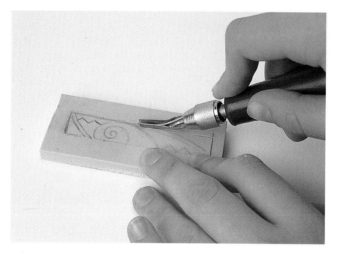

2 Use a V-shaped cutting tool to carve the lines of the design following the manufacturer's instructions for carving. This carving will serve as the mold for the reversed raised edges needed on the silver clay. The raised areas surround and form the cavities for the epoxy resin.

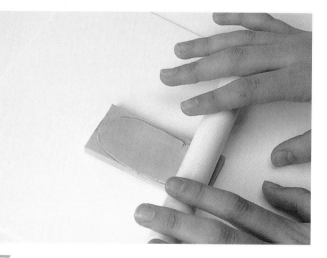

3 Roll out a sheet of clay about 2mm thick. Lightly oil the clay and the carved mold to prevent sticking. Press the sheet of clay onto the mold, and roll again to make sure the clay is in full contact with the surface of the mold.

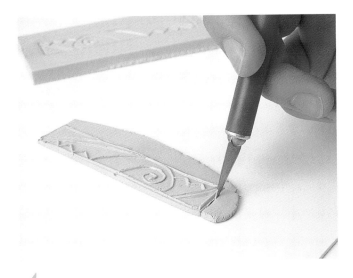

4 Lift the clay from the carved mold and trim around the edges, making any repairs necessary. Let the clay dry. Sand the edges lightly with a nail file to smooth the edges. Place the piece flat on a kiln shelf and fire (PMC®=1650°F for 2 hours). Finish the silver metal piece with a brass brush and sanding papers. For a brighter finish, continue polishing with progressively finer polishing papers or tumbling to a mirror finish.

5 Mix several colors of epoxy resin enamel. Start by mixing equal parts of a hardener and the resin (Envirotex Lite®). Add pigment powders to color the resin. Make sure mixtures are carefully measured and stirred according to the manufacturer's instructions.

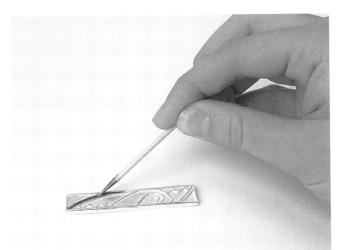

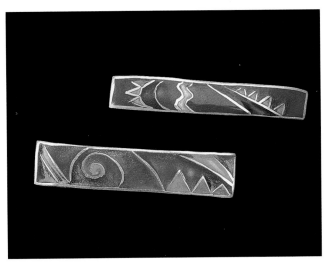

6 Fill the cavities of the finished silver with the colored resin using a toothpick or old paintbrush to apply. Let the piece cure in a warm place for at least 24 hours or until hard to the touch. If it is tacky, let the piece continue to cure.

The finished piece can be left as is or sanded for a matte finish. Sand in water using progressively fine grits of wet/dry sandpapers. Start with 220 grit working up to 600 or higher. Finish with buffing and polishing to bring the shine back. Use clear epoxy resin to glue a tie clip finding to the back.

Photos, color copies, and other paper images shine through clear resin. Personalized bracelets or necklaces are made using vintage clip art images and old family photos. Pigment powders are added to resin to add color to metal. Glass stones can be set into uncured resin for extra sparkle and dimension.

Heritage pin by Carolee Strong. Made with PMC® Silver, photo, epoxy resin, and base metal pin back. *Photo: Dan Haab*

Happy Birthday charm bracelet by Sherri Haab. Made with PMC® Silver, paper images, epoxy resin, and sterling silver chain. *Photo: Dan Haab*

Enamel cat and dog pins by Sherri Haab. Made with Art Clay® Silver, epoxy resin, Pearl Ex pigment powders, and base metal pin backs. *Photo: Dan Haab*

Enamel bars on chain by Sherri Haab. Made with Art Clay® Silver, epoxy resin, Pearl Ex pigment powders, a sterling chain, and a glass rhinestone. *Photo: Dan Haab*

Polymer Clay

Using polymer clay is a great way to incorporate color into your metal clay work. Polymer clay can be sculpted, and will remain soft and pliable until it is baked to harden. A variety of techniques have been developed that can be used to simulate many materials, including stone, wood, glass, and metal. It can be carved, sanded, and buffed or left as is after baking.

Polymer clay must be conditioned after opening the package. To condition the clay, you knead it with your hands until it is soft. A favorite tool of polymer clay artists is a pasta roller, used to roll nice even sheets of varying thicknesses. This tool should be dedicated for use with polymer clay and should not come into contact with any food handling items.

Bake polymer clay on a glass baking dish, or a ceramic tile, in an oven. For those who use polymer clay frequently, it's best to use a toaster oven dedicated just for that. Most brands can be baked at 275° for 30 minutes. Let the clay cool in the oven for a stronger finished product. *Polymer clay emits toxic fumes if fired above the temperature given by the manufacturer's instructions.*

Polymer clay and metal clay look wonderful when combined in a piece. Uncured polymer clay can be baked directly onto finished silver. The silver will be very hot after baking, as it conducts heat well. After the pieces are finished, you can finish the polymer and silver together with sanding and buffing. Since polymer clay is softer than silver, it's helpful to complete most of the silver finishing before adding the polymer clay. Save the final polishing until after the polymer clay has been cured.

Simulating Cloisonné

Cloisonné is a type of enameling. To make faux cloisonné, choose simple graphic designs. Look in clip-art books, graphic design books or rubber stamp catalogs for inspiration. Designs can be simplified and changed by hand or on a copier. You can experiment with colored pencils on copies until you are pleased with your design.

What you need to make this cloisonné pin:

Art Clay® Silver
   (Clay Type)
Basic metal clay tools
   (see pages 18–19)
Rubber stamp block
   (Speedy Stamp™
   Block-Speedball®
   Art Products; see
   Resources)
Speedball® #2 V-shaped
   medium line cutter (see
   Resources)
Premo™ Polymer clay
   (red, yellow, blue; see
   Resources)
Polymer clay tools,
   including pasta roller
   (not to be used for food)
Sobo® white glue

1 Transfer a pencil drawing by rubbing the design face down on a rubber stamp block. Carve the design deeply with a V-shaped cutter into the rubber block. Coat the carved rubber block with olive oil using a paintbrush. Make sure to oil all of the grooves in the carving to keep the clay from sticking.

2 Roll out a thick sheet of silver clay. Press the sheet of clay onto the mold, and roll again to make sure the clay is in full contact with the surface of the mold.

3 Peel the silver clay away from the carving. Use an X-Acto® blade to trim around the edges. Add loops of clay onto the bottom of the pin with slip, if you desire. Dry the pin on a flat surface until bone-dry. Sand the edges with a nail file and make any repairs necessary.

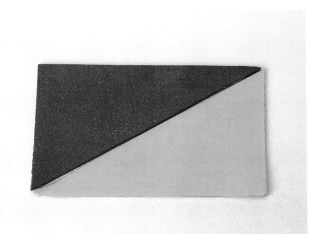

4 Fire the pin as directed for Art Clay® Silver, either in a kiln or by torch-firing (Art Clay® Silver=1600°F for 10 minutes), following instructions on page 28 if torch-firing. Finish with a brass brush and polishing papers. Coat the cavities or cells of the pin with Sobo glue to help the polymer clay stick. Let the glue dry.

5 Make easy polymer clay gradients using a technique known as a Skinner blend (developed by Judith Skinner). Make one combination each of red/yellow, red/blue, and blue/yellow for 3 gradient sheets of clay. To make a Skinner blend, roll out each color of clay in the pasta roller at a #1 setting. Cut rectangles of each color about 4″ by 2½″, and then cut the them diagonally. Combine two colors to form a rectangle. Press the seam to adhere the colors together.

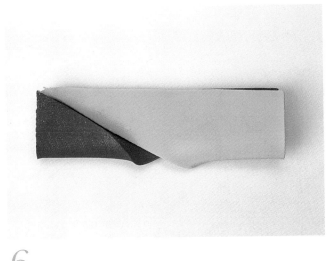

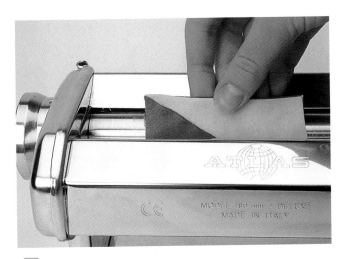

6 Fold the polymer rectangle in half while holding the rectangle horizontally.

7 Run the folded polymer clay rectangle through the pasta roller at a #1 setting, again holding the clay horizontally.

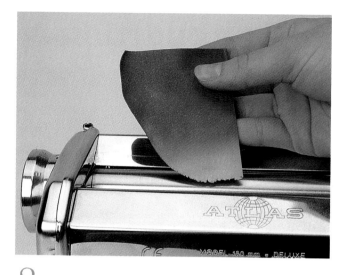

8 Fold (always in the same direction) and run through the pasta roller repeatedly, until a gradient forms. It may take 10 times or more. Repeat with the other polymer clay combinations. Finish rolling when you are pleased with the gradient.

9 Use an X-Acto® blade to cut out shapes of polymer clay to fit into the cavities on the finished silver metal clay pin. Use your fingers or a clay shaper tool to push the clay into the cells. Trim away any excess polymer clay that rises above raised walls of the cells.

10 Bake the pin with the polymer clay in a toaster oven (Art Clay® Silver=275°F for 30 minutes). Let the pin cool. Sand the pin in water with wet/dry sandpaper working progressively from 400 to 600 in grit. For more shine work up to 800 and then 1000 grit papers (800–1000 grit papers are available at auto body supply stores).

Buff the pin on a muslin wheel or with a buffing cloth. If using
a buffing wheel, be careful not to mar the polymer clay, as it is
softer than the silver. Attach a pin-back finding using epoxy
glue. Hang beads onto the loops for a decorative finish.

Mokumé Gané Technique

Mokumé gané is Japanese metal working process. With this technique, different kinds of metal are combined to look like wood grain. This can be simulated with polymer clay, using layers of clay, paint, and metal leaf to achieve interesting effects. Layers are stacked, manipulated, and sliced to reveal textural patterns in the clay.

What you need to make this mokumé gané pendant:

PMC+®

Basic metal clay tools (see pages 18–19)

Premo™ Polymer Clay (one 2 oz. package each of beige, white pearl, gold, and translucent)

Acrylic paint (metallic copper, metallic green, and metallic violet)

Composition metal leaf

Polymer clay tools including a tissue blade and a pasta roller (not to be used for food)

White glue (Sobo®, Elmer's®)

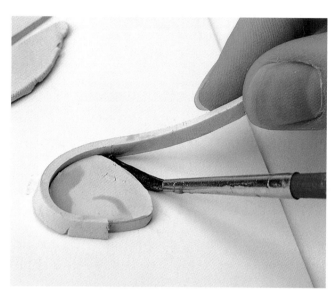

1 Roll out a sheet of PMC+® about 2mm thick. Cut out a base shape (drop shape) for the pendant. Cut long strips out of the sheet ³/₁₆″ wide. Apply water or thin slip to the edges of the pendant, and wrap a strip of clay around the pendant to make a bezel. Cut the ends of the strip to make a butt joint. Join the seam with water and more slip.

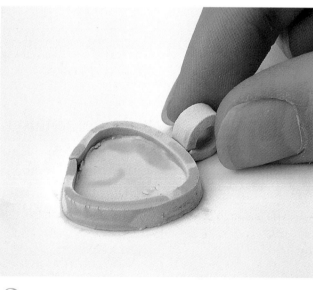

2 Make a loop for the top of the pendant with another strip of clay. Attach the loop with slip. Let the pendant dry until it holds its shape.

3 Add small balls of clay with thick slip around the bezel. Dry the pendant. Sand the surface of the bezel with a nail file. Fire the pendant on a kiln shelf (PMC+®=1650°F for 10 minutes). Finish with a brass brush and polishing paper to desired finish.

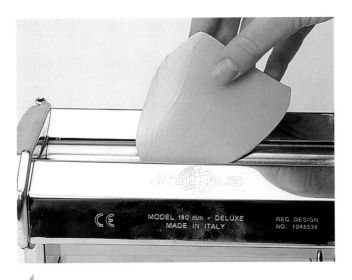

4 Condition the polymer clay (2-oz. packages of beige, white pearl, and gold) by kneading it to soften. Roll each color of polymer clay through the pasta roller on a #1 setting to make sheets. Make 1 sheet of each color and 4 sheets of translucent clay.

5 Trim each sheet into a square with a knife. Paint 3 sheets with metallic paints, using a different color on each one. Apply metal leaf to the unpainted sheet of translucent clay. Let the paint dry.

6 Stack the sheets of clay in the following order, starting with the bottom: translucent with metal leaf, white pearl, green painted translucent, gold clay, beige, violet painted translucent, and then copper painted translucent.

7 Use a roller to compact the stack of clay, and flatten slightly. Roll the stack through the pasta roller. Cut the sheet in half.

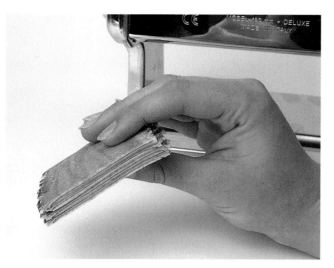

8 Stack the cut pieces together, and roll the stack back through the pasta roller. Cut and repeat the process of restacking the clay layers 2–3 more times.

9 After the final pass through the pasta roller, cut several squares (about 2″ square) out of the rolled sheet of clay, and stack them until they are about 1-inch thick. Place the stack on a base of scrap clay. Press it firmly on a work surface until it sticks. Push texturing tools deeply into the top of the clay. A pastry wheel was used to make this texture.

10 Cut thin slices from the top surface of the block of clay with a long tissue blade, starting at one corner and slicing to the opposite corner. Continue slicing the clay to make several thin layers of mokumé gané clay.

11 Roll out a background sheet of white pearl translucent clay in the pasta roller at the #1 setting. Apply a slice of the mokumé gané to the pearl white clay. Roll the clay through the pasta roller at the #1 setting just once to bond the layer to the background sheet.

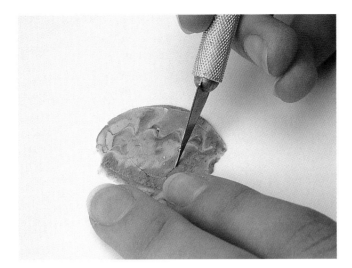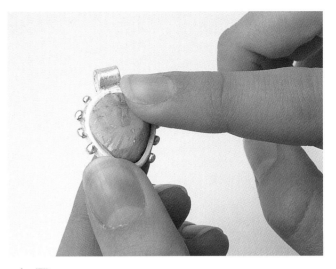

12 Paint a thin layer of white glue inside of metal clay bezel. Let the glue dry. Cut out a shape of mokumé gané polymer clay to fit into the finished metal clay bezel.

13 Press the edges of the polymer clay to fit tightly into the bezel.

Bake the pendant once more in an oven (polymer clay=275°F for 30 minutes). Sand the surface of the polymer clay under water with wet/dry sandpaper. Start with 400-grit paper working up to 600, then use 800–1000 grit if you want a higher shine. Buff with muslin on a buffing wheel or with a soft cloth by hand.

Applying Gold Leaf to Polymer Clay

Use polymer clay to create custom designer jewelry to match the style or color of an outfit. You can use bold colors and gold leaf to make a striking piece. Pattern and texture applied to polymer clay will change the way the clay reflects light. This heart pin features a contemporary look with a checkerboard design created using gold leaf.

What you need to make this checkered heart necklace:

PMC+®

Basic metal clay tools (see pages 18–19)

Premo™ polymer clay (one 2-oz. package each of red pearl and yellow)

Polymer clay tools, tissue blade, and pasta roller (not to be used for food)

Gold leaf sheet or composition leaf

Sobo® glue

1 Follow the instructions on page 126 (mokumé gané pendant steps 1–3) to make the bezel. Instead of a drop shape in step 1, cut the base sheet of metal clay into a heart shape. Coat the finished heart bezel with Sobo® glue. Condition a 2-oz. block of red pearl clay, and roll through the pasta roller at the #1 setting.

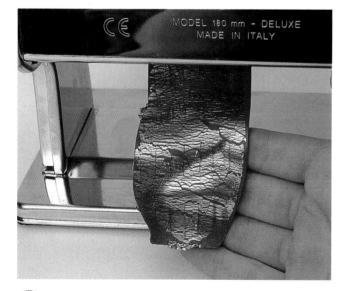

2 Apply a sheet of gold leaf over the surface of the sheet of polymer clay. Roll the clay with the leaf through the pasta roller at the #3 setting. Run the sheet again through the pasta roller on #5. The gold leaf will appear crackled on the surface.

3 Use a long tissue blade to cut thin strips of the clay, about 1/8″ wide. Make a background sheet, using a lighter shade of red clay or make a gradient with yellow and red (see page 123, Cloisonné pin steps 5–8). Roll it at the #3 setting on the pasta roller. Apply the strips onto a background sheet of clay, leaving 1/8″ space between each strip.

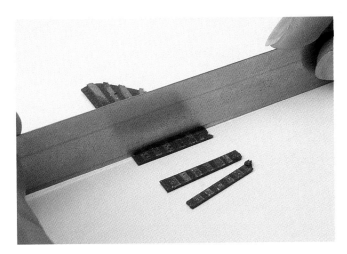

4 After the strips of clay are applied to the background piece, roll the sheet—with the stripes vertically positioned—through the pasta roller at the #3 or #4 setting (enough to flatten the strips of clay onto the background). Cut across the sheet horizontally to make $1/8''$ strips from the sheet.

5 Roll out a scrap piece of red clay in the pasta roller at the #1 setting to make the background. Lay the cut strips onto it to form a checkerboard pattern. Press or roll the strips lightly with a roller onto the background clay.

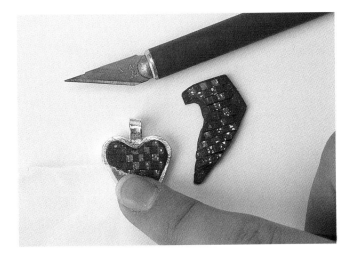

6 Cut out a heart shape from the checkered polymer clay sheet and press into the bezel.

Bake the heart pendant a second time in an oven (polymer clay=275°F for 30 minutes).

Polymer Clay Gallery

Polymer clay is one of the most exciting and versatile art mediums in use today. Artists have developed signature styles in mixed media pieces combining polymer clay and metal clay. These pieces were made using a variety of different techniques and surface treatments featuring polymer clay.

▼ *Neck Jest* by Wendy Wallin Malinow. Made using PMC®, with polymer clay inlay. *Photo: Courtney Frisse*

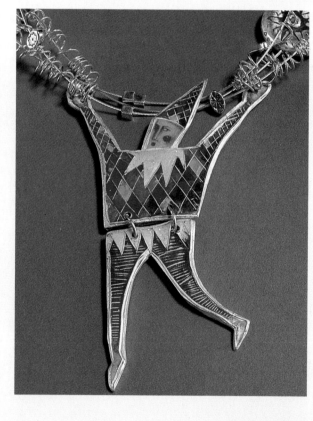

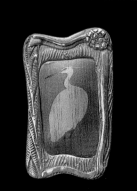

▶ *Crane Pendant* by Eileen Loring. Made using PMC+®, with Lazertran image transferred onto polymer clay. *Photo: Dan Haab*

▲ *I Want Candy* by Wendy Wallin Malinow. Made with PMC®, polymer clay inlay, resin, and sterling silver. *Photo: Courtney Frisse*

Glass

Glass and glass enamels are mediums that work well with metal clay. Certain types of glass can be incorporated with unfired silver metal clay or applied to finished silver as you would for enameling. PMC3® and Art Clay® Silver 650 metal clays work especially well, because they fire at lower temperatures than the other types of metal clay. These temperatures are compatible with the temperatures needed to heat and anneal the glass without melting it into a pool in the kiln.

Silver metal clay is ideal for enameling, because it is fine silver. Fine silver has a beautiful pure color that shines through transparent glass enamels. You can texture metal clay with rubber stamps or other objects before it is fired to create "cells" to fill with enamel, which is easier than the traditional method. The finished piece simulates cloisonné and basse-taille enameling. Using metal clay opens the door for new methods and surface treatments to which enamels can be applied.

Some considerations need to be taken into account when working with glass. The glass project in this book was made with a small-to-medium-sized dichroic glass cabochon. This glass is very easy to incorporate into a PMC3® or Art Clay® Silver 650 metal clay project, as the firing process for both the metal and the glass are compatible. It is important to understand the properties of glass so that you will be successful in all of your glass/metal projects.

All glass is sensitive to heat. If glass is heated or cooled too quickly, it will crack. The kiln must be ramped up at a rate that allows the glass to adjust to the heat. After firing the piece, the glass must be cooled slowly to prevent thermal shock from cracking it. This can be accomplished by leaving the kiln door shut until the glass piece has cooled completely.

Glass must be annealed when it is heated or fired. Annealing stabilizes the glass to prevent strain on it and is accomplished through proper heating and cooling. Annealing temperatures and length of annealing times are determined by the type of glass used, and by the thickness of the glass. Larger pieces need to be annealed for longer periods of time. Refer to annealing charts provided by glass manufacturers.

If glass is held at high temperatures and for long enough, it can cause devitrification. This causes the surface of the glass to become cloudy and rough as the glass changes to a crystalline condition. Most types of glass used for kiln work are formulated to minimize the chance of devitrification.

Using the proper glass, combined with the use of PMC3® or Art Clay® Silver 650, leaves little chance of failure. As long as you use low temperatures and monitor the heating and cooling of the glass, you should be successful with your projects.

Dichroic glass cabochons are great to use if you want to combine glass with metal clay. They have a surface layer consisting of fine metal particles. The surface color has an iridescent quality that appears differently depending on which angle you are viewing it from. To make cabochons, layers of dichroic glass are fused together and annealed to make "gemlike" shapes out of the glass. Dichroic glass cabochons made with Bullseye or Uroboros® glass can easily be fired with silver metal clay. Metal clay can be used to surround a cabochon to make bezels that frame the glass, and both can be fired together to make jewelry or functional items emphasizing the beauty of the dichroic glass.

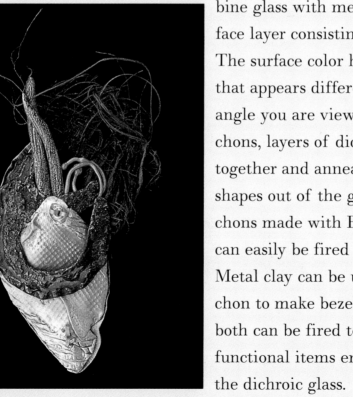

See Life pin, by Carl Stanley. Made with PMC® Silver, enamel, sterling silver, 14K gold/palm fiber. The artist applied glass enamel to the surface of the metal clay form. Other metals and fibers were added for depth and interest. *Photo: Patrick Flannery*

Firing Glass with Metal Clay

Glass artists who specialize in making dichroic glass cabochons combine color and pattern to create beautiful combinations. Choosing a glass cabochon can give you inspiration for designing a metal clay project. This bookmark is a way to make something other than jewelry and a great way to feature glass in your work.

What you need to make a dichroic glass bookmark:

PMC3®

Basic metal clay supplies (see pages 18–19)

Texturing tools

3/4"–1" dichroic glass cabochon

Bullseye ThinFire Paper

2" piece of 20-gauge sterling silver wire

5/8" wide ribbon, 12" long

1 Roll out a sheet of PMC3® the thickness of a mat board. Texture the clay with an object or texturing tools, such as the shell in this photo.

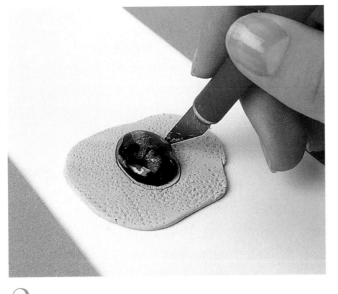

2 Place the dichroic cabochon in the center of the sheet of clay, and cut around the cabochon using a sharp knife.

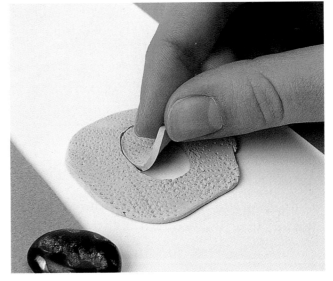

3 Remove the center piece of clay to make a bezel. Replace the cabochon. The clay will shrink around the glass.

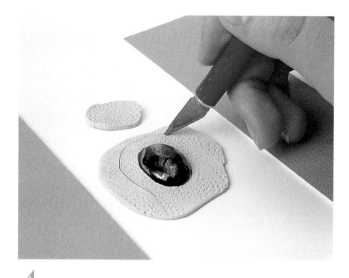

4   Trim the clay to make a border at least ¼" to frame the cabochon. It can be cut any shape. You can use the design of the cabochon for inspiration.

5   Roll a skinny snake of clay and moisten it with water. Place it around the cabochon for a loose fit. Drape the rope around the cabochon without stretching or pulling the clay to fit. Cut the ends bluntly, and seal them with water to join. Smooth the seam well for a strong bezel.

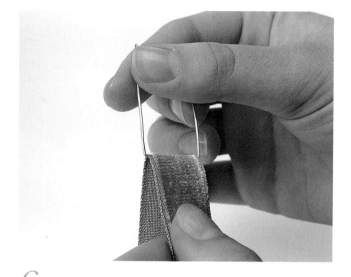

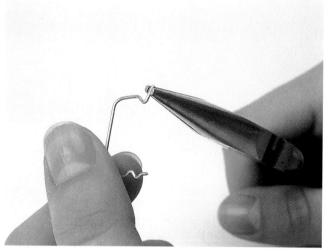

6   Bend the sterling silver wire to fit the width of the ribbon (¾").

7   Bend the wire on each side to anchor the wire embedded in the clay. Clip off excess wire on each side.

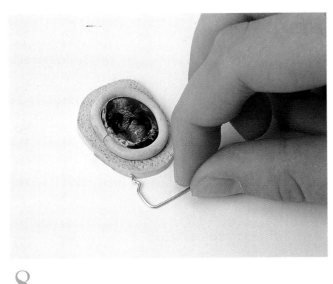

8 Push the wire well into the clay, leaving enough room to loop the ribbon through after firing.

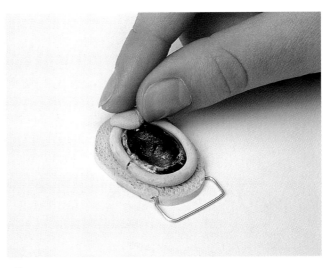

9 Embellish the bezel with small pieces of clay, attaching with water and using texturing tools to decorate. Let the piece dry completely. Use a nail file to smooth edges.

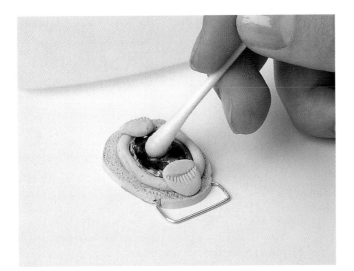

10 Clean the glass cabochon with a cotton swab dipped in rubbing alcohol to clean the surface. Make sure you remove dust and fingerprints. Follow the firing directions on the right.

Firing the Dichroic Glass Bookmark

Hold the piece by the edges, to keep the glass clean, and place on a piece of Bullseye ThinFire paper on a flat kiln shelf. The paper will keep the back of the cabochon smooth as it fires. Caution: Do not fire the glass with a torch, as it could shatter, sending glass pieces flying. Use a kiln, following all safety precautions and wearing eye protection when opening it.

Set the ramp speed of the kiln to 1500°F per hour (for a cabochon that is about ¹/₃" thick). This is slow enough to heat the glass uniformly to prevent cracking. Fire the piece at 1290°F for 10 minutes. For small and medium-sized cabochons, you can turn off the kiln at this point and keep the door shut until they are completely cooled. The firing, plus retained heat in the kiln during cooling, should be sufficient to anneal a small dichroic cabochon.

For large cabochons, a longer annealing time may be required; refer to the manufacturer's information.

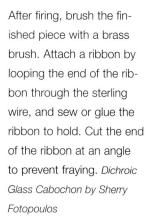

After firing, brush the finished piece with a brass brush. Attach a ribbon by looping the end of the ribbon through the sterling wire, and sew or glue the ribbon to hold. Cut the end of the ribbon at an angle to prevent fraying. *Dichroic Glass Cabochon by Sherry Fotopoulos*

Glass adds sparkle and color to metal clay. Glass cabochons are fired into place with metal clay bezels surrounding the glass. Glass enamel powder applied to the surface of fine silver is used create colorful cloisonné pieces. Glass and glass enamel offer a variety of techniques available to use with silver metal clay.

Galaxy Necklace by Melanie Bentley Shockley. This was handsculpted with PMC3® and handmade dichroic glass cabochon. It was strung on "soft touch" cable with kishi pearls and Czech seed beads. *Photo: Bowyers Studio*

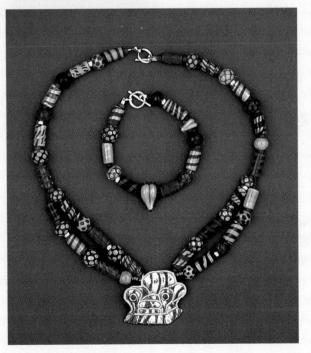

Chinese Zen Necklace by Melanie Bentley Shockley. This was handsculpted using PMC3® and features an organically hued glass cabochon in the center, embedded sterling findings, white kishi pearls, and sterling wires. The pendant is displayed with copper biwa pearls on "soft touch" cable. *Photo: Bowyers Studio*

Blue Striped Easy Chair by Barbara Becker Simon. Cloisonné technique using glass enamel. *Photo: Robert Diamante*

Contributing Artists

Dan Barney
Orem, UT
801-224-9992
boudiccaart@hotmail.com

Chris Darway
PMC® Tool and Supply
1 Feeder Street
Lambertville, NJ 08530
609-397-9550
609-397-0702 (fax)
darwaydesign@earthlink.net

Sherry Fotopoulos
PMC Connection
Senior Instructor
www.pmc123.com

Dawn Hale
1-866-735-0600
www.dawnhaledesign.com

Eileen Loring
Windsor, CO
ejloring@attbi.com

Wendy Wallin Malinow
10815 SW Southridge Drive
Portland, OR 97219
503-697-3877

Kate Ferrant Richbourg, Instructor
800 N. El Camino Real #102
San Mateo, CA 94401
415-518-6766

Melanie Bentley Shockley
Aruru Clayworks
3801 Stanford Court
Midlothian, Virginia 23113
804-327-1666
www.aruruclayworks.com

Barbara Becker Simon
midas@iline.com
www.bbsimon.com

Carl Stanley
1744 Calle Poniente
Santa Barbara, CA 93101
805-687-5415

Carolee Strong
quiltracer@aol.com
Springville, UT

Shahasp Valentine
415-920-9439
www.precieux.com

Candice Wakumoto
P.O. Box 893113
Mililani, HI   96789
(808) 625-2706
candicewakumoto@msn.com

Resources

Metal Clay and Metal Clay Supplies

Art Clay World, USA
4535 Southwest Highway
Oak Lawn, IL 60453
866-381-0100
708-857-8800
708-636-5408 (fax)
www.artclayworld.com

JEC Products Inc.
P.O. Box 552
Port Byron, IL 61275
309-523-2600
www.jecproducts.com
Ultra Lite Kilns

MetalClay
P.O. Box 14928
Albuquerque, NM 87191-4928
505-332-9245
www.metalclay.com
mail@metalclay.com

New Mexico Clay
3300 Girard NE
Albuquerque, NM 87107
800-781-2529
505-881-2350
www.nmclay.com

PMC® Connection
3718 Cavalier Drive
Garland, TX 75042
866-PMC-CLAY
972-485-0200
www.pmcconnection.com

PMC® Tool and Supply
1 Feeder Street
Lambertville, NJ 08530
609-397-9550
609-397-0702 (fax)
darwaydesign@earthlink.net

Rio Grande
7500 Bluewater Road
Albuquerque, NM 87121
800-443-6766
505-839-3011 (international accounts)
505-839-3016 (fax)
www.riogrande.com
PMC® tools, kiln supplies, videos

Please read both sides before signing.

1. **Consent to Treatment.** I consent to the provision of medical care required to treat the condition for which I am being admitted to the Hospital, including routine diagnostic procedures and other medical treatments ordered by my physician or other healthcare professional on the Hospital's medical staff. I understand that, absent emergency or extraordinary circumstances, major medical or surgical procedures will not be performed upon me unless and until I have had an opportunity to discuss the risks and benefits of the procedure or treatment with the physician or other healthcare professional. I understand that it is the treating healthcare professional's responsibility to obtain my informed consent, and that I have the right to consent, or to refuse consent to a proposed procedure or therapeutic course after discussion with the treating healthcare professional.

Acknowledged: _____ (initial)

2. **Patient Self-Determination Act.** I have been offered information regarding Advance Directives (such as durable powers of attorney for healthcare and living wills), and have been informed that I may receive a copy of this information at any time during my hospital stay. I have been informed that a Patient Handbook containing patient rights and responsibilities and other information relating to my stay is available to me in Patient Registration or at my request during my hospital stay. **Please initial the following applicable statements:**

I have executed an Advance Directive and have been requested to supply a copy to the Hospital. _____
I have not executed an Advance Directive at this time. _____
I wish to execute an Advance Directive at this time. _____
I do not wish to execute an Advance Directive at this time. _____

3. **Notice of Privacy Practices.** I acknowledge that I have received the Hospital's Notice of Privacy Practices, which describes the ways in which the Hospital will use and disclose my healthcare information for treatment, payment, healthcare operations and other described and permitted uses and disclosures. I understand that I may contact the Hospital Privacy Official designated on the Notice if I have a complaint.
Acknowledged: _____ (Initial)

4. **Payment:** I permit the Hospital and the physicians or other health professionals involved in my inpatient or outpatient care to release the healthcare information necessary to facilitate payment by a person or entity liable for payment on my behalf to such person or entity in order to verify coverage or payment questions, or for any other purpose related to benefit payment. If I am a Medicare or Medicaid patient, I authorize the release of healthcare information to the Social Security Administration or its intermediaries or carriers for payment of a Medicare claim or to the appropriate state agency for payment of a Medicaid claim. This information may include, without limitation, history and physical, emergency records, laboratory reports, operative reports, physician progress notes, nurses notes, consultations, psychological and/or psychiatric reports and discharge summary. This consent specifically includes information concerning psychological conditions, psychiatric conditions, and/or infectious diseases, including, but not limited to, blood-borne diseases such as Hepatitis, Human Immunodeficiency Virus (HIV) and Acquired Immune Deficiency Syndrome (AIDS).

Acknowledged: _____ (Initial)

5. **Assignment of Benefits.** In executing this assignment of benefits, I am directing the health insurance carrier or other health benefit plan providing my coverage to pay the Hospital and/or hospital-based physicians* directly for the services the Hospital and/or hospital-based physicians provide to me, my minor child, or other person entitled to health care benefits for this admission. In return for the services rendered and to be rendered by the Hospital and/or hospital-based physicians, I hereby irrevocably assign and transfer to the Hospital and/or hospital-based physicians all right, title, and interest in all benefits payable for the healthcare rendered, which are provided in any and all insurance polices and health benefit plans from which my dependents or I are entitled to recover. This assignment and transfer shall be for the

All sections, front and back, are incorporated by reference herein.

I hereby certify that I have read and understand this Conditions of Admission and Consent for Medical Treatment Form, and I have signed this document knowingly, freely, and voluntarily. Moreover, I certify and state that I have received no promises, assurances, or guarantees from anyone as to the results that may be obtained by any medical treatment or services.

☐ Patient is medically unable to sign the Conditions of Admissions

Patient/Parent/Guardian/Conservator	If other than patient, indicate relationship
X	
Spouse (if married/available)	Witness (to Signature only)
X	X
	PATIENT IDENTIFICATION

Date ___8/7/04___   Time ___1:17___ ☐ a.m. ☐ p.m.

Conditions of Admission and Consent for Medical Treatment

A7414 05/03   Page 1 of 2   PATIENT COPY

purpose of granting the Hospital and/or hospital-based physicians an independent right of recovery against my insurer or health benefit plan, but shall not be construed as an obligation of the Hospital and/or hospital-based physicians to pursue any such right of recovery. In no event will the Hospital retain benefits in excess of the amount owed to the Hospital for the care and treatment rendered during the admission. I have read and been given the opportunity to ask questions about this assignment of benefits, and I have signed this document freely and without inducement, other than the rendition of services by the Hospital.

6. **Financial Agreement.** In consideration of the services to be rendered to the patient, the undersigned individual (as parent, guardian, spouse, guarantor, agent or as the patient) promises to pay the patient's account at the rates stated in the Hospital's price list (known as the "Charge Master") effective on the date the charge is processed for the service provided, which rates are hereby expressly incorporated by reference as the price term of this Agreement to pay the patient's account. Some special items will be priced separately if the charge is listed as zero. In the event that the Hospital has to engage an attorney or collection agency to collect any unpaid balances that arise from the treatment consented to herein, the undersigned agrees to pay the reasonable attorney's fees and collection expenses incurred by the Hospital.

    An estimate of the anticipated charges for services to be provided to the patient is available upon request from the Hospital. Estimates may vary significantly from the final charges based on a variety of factors, including but not limited to the course of treatment, intensity of care, physician practices, and the necessity of providing additional goods and services.

    The Hospital will provide a medical screening examination to all patients who are seeking emergency medical services to determine if there is an emergency medical condition, without regard to the patient's ability to pay. If there is an emergency medical condition, the Hospital will provide stabilizing treatment. However, patients are not relieved of their obligation to pay for these services if they have the ability to pay.

7. **Patient Rights.** I acknowledge that I have been given information and instructions regarding my Patient Rights, which include, but are not limited to, the right to make medical decisions, including the right to accept or refuse medical treatment, to participate in my plan of care and to receive care in a safe setting, free from verbal or physical abuse or harassment. I acknowledge that I have also received information about the Hospital's grievance process.

8. **Private Room.** I understand and agree that the patient or the party responsible for payment for hospital and medical services is responsible for any additional charges associated with the request and use of a private room.

9. **Communications About My Healthcare.** I authorize my healthcare information to be disclosed for purposes of communicating results, findings, and care decisions to my family members and others responsible for my care or designated by me. I will provide those individuals with a password or other verification means specified by the Hospital.

* *Hospital-based physicians include (but are not limited to): Emergency Room Physicians, Pathologists, Radiologists, and Anesthesiologists. These services are not part of your hospital bill and will be billed separately by their companies.*

10. **Medicare Patient Certification and Assignment of Benefits.** I certify that the information I provide in applying for payment under Title XVIII (Medicare) or Title XIX (Medicaid) of the Social Security Act is correct. I request payment of authorized benefits to be made on my behalf to the Hospital or hospital-based physician by the Medicare or Medicaid Program.

11. **Other Acknowledgements.**

     a. Legal Relationship Between Hospital and Physicians. I acknowledge and agree that neither this Hospital nor any outpatient department, clinic, or other healthcare entity operated as part of this Hospital to which I may be transferred or in which I may be treated is responsible for the judgment or conduct of any physician who treats or provides a professional service to me. I acknowledge and understand that each physician providing services at the Hospital is an independent contractor who is self-employed and is not the agent, servant, or employee of Hospital. I further understand that other physicians may be called upon to provide care, either directly (as consultants) or indirectly through professional services (i.e., radiology, pathology, EKG interpretation, anesthesiology). These physicians are also independent contractors who are self-employed and are not the agents, servants, or employees of Hospital. I acknowledge and understand that for emergency or unscheduled services, the Hospital may aid my selection of physicians by an established "on-call" roster provided through each department of the Hospital. These physicians are also independent contractors who are self-employed and are not the agents, servants, or employees of Hospital. I further agree that Hospital is not responsible for the judgment or conduct of any of the physicians identified above.

     b. Personal Valuables. I understand that the Hospital maintains a safe for the safekeeping of money and valuables, and the Hospital shall not be liable for the loss of or damage to any money, jewelry, documents, furs, fur coats and fur garments, or other articles of unusual value and small size, unless placed in the safe, and shall not be liable for loss or damage to any other personal property, unless deposited with the Hospital for safekeeping.

     c. Weapons/Explosives/Drugs. I understand and agree that if the Hospital at any time believes there may be a weapon, explosive device, illegal substance or drug, or any alcoholic beverage in my room or with my belongings, the Hospital may search my room and my belongings, confiscate any of the above items that are found, and dispose of them as appropriate, including delivery of any item to law enforcement authorities.

Continue reading and sign on reverse side.

Polymer Clay and Supplies

Clay Factory Inc.
P.O. Box 460598
Escondido, CA 92046-0598
877-728-5739
www.clayfactoryinc.com
Polymer clay, ripple blades, pattern cutters, tools, general supplies

Polyform Products
1901 Estes Elk Grove Village, IL 60007
polyform@sculpey.com
Sculpey™ clay products

Polymer Clay Express
13017 Wisteria Drive Box 275
Germantown, MD 20874
301-482-0435
800-844-0158
www.polymerclayexpress.com
Polymer Clay, clay shapers, blades and clay cutters, findings and tools

Prairie Craft
P.O. Box 209
Florissant, CO 80816
800-779-0615
www.prairiecraft.com
Polymer clay, Kato NuBlade™, tools, pattern cutters, Dockyard carving tools

Molding and Casting Supplies

Microsonic, Inc.
1421 Merchant Street
Ambridge, PA 15003
800-523-7672
724-266-9270
724-266-6309 (fax)
www.earmolds.com
Mega-sil™

Silpak
470 East Bonita Ave.
Pomona, CA 91767
909-625-0056
www.silpak.com
Silputty®-40

WFR/Aquaplast Corporation
30 Lawlins Park
Wyckoff, NJ 07481
800-526-5247
201-891-1042
www.wfr-aquaplast.com
Protoplast™ (Thermoplastic Molding Material)

Adhesives and Epoxy Resin

Delta Technical Coating Inc.
800-423-4135
Sobo® glue

Environmental Technologies Inc.
South Bay Depot Rd
P.O. Box 365
Fields Landing, CA 95537-0365
707-443-9323
707-443-7962 (fax)
www.eti-usa.com
Envirotex Lite®
Two-part epoxy resin

Plaid Enterprises, Inc.
3225 Westech Dr.
Norcross, GA 30092
800-842-4197
www.plaidonline.com
Mod Podge®—decoupage glue

Rio Grande
(see Metal Clay and Metal Clay Supplies)

Jewelry Findings

Fire Mountain Gems™
One Fire Mountain Way
Grants Pass, OR 97526-2373
800-355-2137
www.firemountaingems.com
Beads, findings, stringing supplies, books

Sherry Fotopoulos
PMC Connection Senior Instructor
www.pmc123.com
Dichroic glass, PMC® supplies, books

Michele McManus
www.epiphany-art.com
303-394-9033
Dichroic glass cabochons, jewelry

Metalliferous Inc.
34 West 46th St.
New York, NY 10036
888-944-0909
www.metalliferous.com
Jewelry findings, wire, tools and supplies

Thunderbird Supply Co.
1907 West Hwy 66
Gallup, NM 87301
505-722-4323
505-722-6736 (fax)
or
2311 Vassar
Albuquerque, NM 87107-1827
505-884-9427
505-884-6936 (fax)
www.tbscorp.com
Orders:
800-545-7968
Jewelry findings, beads, and tools

Rio Grande
(see Metal Clay and Metal Clay
Supplies)
Jewelry findings and stones

Craft Supplies and Tools

Craft Supplies USA
1287 East 1120 South
Provo, UT 84606
801-373-0919
Project kit for Perfume Holder Kit
#0507043, brass tubing kits for letter
openers, pen making kits, mirrors, key
chains

Harbor Freight Tools
800-444-3353
www.harborfreight.com
Metal stamping tools, hand and power
tools

Jacquard Products/Rupert Gibbon
& Spider Inc.
www.jacquardproducts.com
707-433-9577
Pearl Ex Pigment Powders, craft kits

Kemper Tools
800-388-5367
www.kempertools.com
Sculpting tools and supplies, Klay
Kutters

Creative Paperclay®
79 Daily Dr., Suite 101
Camarillo, CA 93010
805-484-6648
805-484-8788 (fax)
Air-hardening paper clay

The Leather Factory
800-433-3201
www.tandyleather.com
Leather stamping tools, findings,
leather cord

Micro Mark
340 Snyder Avenue
Berkeley Heights, NJ 07922-1595
908-464-2984
www.micromark.com
Carving tools, drills, adhesives, mold
making supplies

Scratch-Art® Co. Inc.
P.O. Box 303
11 Robbie Rd.
Avon, MA 02322
800-377-9003
www.scratchart.com
Shade-Tex® Rubbing Plates

Speedball® Art Products
2226 Speedball Rd.
Statesville, NC 28677
800-898-7224
www.speedballart.com
V-shaped line cutters, Speedy Stamp™
Blocks

Other Resources

Badger Balm
1-800-603-6100
www.badgerbalm.com

Dover Books
www.doverpublications.com
Clip art books and CD-ROMs, copyright
free illustrations

Organizations and Guilds

National Polymer Clay Guild
1350 Beverly Road
Suite 115-345
McLean, VA 22101
www.npcg.org

PMC® Guild
417 W. Mountain Ave.
Fort Collins, CO 80521
www.pmcguild.com

Index

A

Aida Chemical Industries, 11
Annealing, 133–134
Art Clay Gold, 11, 30, 84, 100
Art Clay Silver
  beads, 71–76
  bezel, 88–89
  boxes, 79–80
  cloisonné pin, 122–125
  cone vase, 81–82
  firing, 30, 84
  glass with, 133
  Paper Type, 17
  pins, 85–87
  products, 11, 16–17, 25
  rings, 93, 94–98
  Sheet Type, 17, 105
  Syringe type, 15, 22–23
Art Clay World, 11
Artichoke beads, 8, 75–76
Attachments, adding, 23, 40

B

Badger Balm, 18
Baisse–taille enameling, 133
Barney, Dan, 68
Beads, 69–77
  cork clay cores, 69–70
  elaborate, 75–76
  gallery, 77
  round, 71–72
  silver metal paper, 111–112
  tube, 73–74
Beveled edges, 95
Bezels, 84, 88–89, 126, 134, 139
Bone–dry clay, 24
Bookmark, dichroic glass, 135–137
Boxes and vessels, 78–83
  cork clay core, 78
  gallery, 83
  lace cone vase, 81–82
  lidded box, 79–80
Bracelets
  carved, 48
  molded, 55–58
  sculpted, 63–67
  silver metal paper, 112, 113
  textured, 39–43
Branch bracelet, 55–58
Brass brushes, 31, 138
Brooches. See Pins
Buffing, 34, 38, 125
Bullseye glass, 134
Burnishing, 31–32, 38, 138
Butterfly pins, 86–87
Button necklace, 50–52
Buttons, 53–54

C

Cabochons, dichroic glass, 16, 133, 134, 135–137
Carving, 45–48
  on dry clay, 46–47
  gallery, 48
  tools, 45
Charm bracelets, 39–41, 63–67
Checkered heart necklace, 130–131
Christmas tree pins, 84–87
Clay cutter, 88
Clay shaper, 18
Cloisonné
  glass enamel, 133, 139
  polymer clay, 122–125
Color pigment, with epoxy resin, 114, 118–119
Cone vase, 81–82
Cookie cutters, 19, 39
Cork clay core, 69–70, 78
Corundums, 84
Creative Paperclay, 27, 69, 70

D

Devitrification, 134
Dichroic glass cabochons, 16, 133, 134, 135–137
Dockyard Micro Carving Tools, 45
Doll prop, 27
Dry clay
  carving on, 46–47
  working with, 24
Drying process
  slowing, 23
  speeding, 24
Drying time, 24

E

Earrings
  gold/silver combination, 101–103
  stone setting, 90
Enamel tie, epoxy resin, 118–119
Epoxy resin, 114–120
  clear, 114, 115–117
  with color pigment, 114, 118–119
  gallery, 120
  resources for, 141

F

Fiber blanket/cloth, 27
Files/filing, 33, 40, 51
Finishing
  buffing, 34, 38, 125
  burnishing, 31–32, 38, 138
  filing and sanding, 33, 40, 51
  patina, 34–35, 38, 44, 91
  soldering, 34
  texture and, 38
  unfired clay, 24–25
Firing
  cork clay core, 69–70, 78
  glass with metal clay, 133–134, 137
  kilns, 26–27, 30, 69, 133, 137
  silver metal paper, 105
  stones, 84–85
  strength after, 29
  stress cracks in, 25
  temperature, 30
  torch–firing, 28, 100, 105, 123
  wet clay and, 24
Flexible molds, 49
Flowers
  gold and silver, 101–103
  sculpted, 61–62
  stone setting, 90–91
Forming techniques, 21–24
Found objects, 18, 23, 38
Fresh wet clay, forming, 21–24

G

Garnets, 84
Glass enamel powder, 139
Glass and glass enamel, 133–139
  bookmark, 135–137
  firing, 133–134, 137
  gallery, 139
Gold, purity of, 9
Gold leaf, with polymer clay, 130–131
Gold metal clay
  Art Clay, 11, 30, 84, 100
  combining with silver, 100, 101–103
  gallery, 104
  PMC, 15, 100
  shrinkage rate, 100
Gold slip, 100

H

Haab, Sherri, 44, 48, 77, 92, 99, 113, 120
Hale, Dawn, 44, 59, 92, 99, 104
Hematite, 84
Hughes, Mary, 8
Hydrating and rehydrating, 19, 20, 21

I

I.D. bracelet, 42–43

J

Jewelry
  carved, 46–48
  epoxy resin, 120
  glass and glass enamel, 139
  gold/silver combination, 101–104
  molded, 50–52, 55–59
  paper punch, 106–107
  polymer clay, 122–132
  resources for, 19, 141–142
  sculpted, 61–67
  stone set, 84–92
  textured, 39–44
  See also specific types
Jewelry tumbler, 32

K

Kiln firing, 26–27, 30, 69, 133, 137

L

Loops, forming, 22
Loring, Eileen, 44, 82, 83, 132

M

Malinow, Wendy Wallin, 132
Mandrel, 93, 95
Mat board, 18
Mat cutting blade, 19
Matte finish, 31
Metal clay
    defined, 9
    resources for, 140–142
    tools and supplies, 18–19
    types of, 11, 14–17
    See also specific techniques
Mitsubishi Materials, 11, 14
Mokumé gané, 126–129
Mold–making, 49–59
    polymer clay, 49, 50–52, 55
    resources for, 141
    silicone, 53–54
    two–part, 55–58
Moonstone, 84

N

Nail file, 33, 40, 51
Necklace
    molded, 50–52
    polymer clay, 130–131
    stone set, 88–89
Needle tool, 18, 40, 64, 70,
    101, 106, 107, 116

O

Oil Paste, 17, 25
Olive oil, 18, 23, 38, 57
Overlay Paste, 17

P

Paper punch, 105, 106–107,
    108
Pasta roller, 121, 123, 124
Paste Type clay, 17, 25
Patina, 34–35, 38, 44, 91
Pattern cutters, 19
Pearl earrings, 90–91
Pendants
    carved, 46–47
    gold/silver combination,

101–103
    polymer clay, 126–129, 132
    sculpted, 61–62
    silver metal paper, 106–107,
    113
Perfume vial, paper punch,
    108–110
Peridot, 84
Petroglyph designs, 46–47, 48
Picture frame, epoxy resin,
    115–117
Pins
    polymer clay, 122–125
    stone setting, 84–87
Pin vise, 24, 40
Plastic wrap, 18
Playing cards, 18, 21
PMC. See Precious Metal Clay
Polishing papers, 33
Polymer clay, 121–132
    baking, 121, 124, 129
    cloisonné, 122–125
    conditioning, 121
    gallery, 132
    gold leaf applied to,
130–131
    mokumé gané, 126–129
    molds, 49, 50–52, 55
    resources for, 141
    silver combination, 121
Precious Metal Clay (PMC)
    carving, 45–48
    with epoxy resin, 115–119
    firing, 30, 84
    with glass, 133, 135–137
    gold, 15, 100
    gold/silver combination,
    101–103
    molding, 50–58
    one–ounce lump, working
    with, 20
    Paper Type, 15, 105,
106–113
    with polymer clay, 126–131
    products, 11, 14–15
    rings, 93
    sculpting, 60–68, 61–62
    stone setting, 90–91
    strength after firing, 29
    texturing, 39–41

R

Repairs, 25
Richbourg, Kate Ferrant,
    10, 77, 113
Rings, 93–99
    gallery, 99
    silverware, 94–96
    stone setting, 97–98
    tools and materials, 93
Rolled clay sheets, 21
Rollers, 18
Ropes, forming, 22
Rose pendant, sculpted, 61–62

S

Sanding, 24, 33, 109
Scratch–brushing, 31
Sculpting, 60–68
    gallery, 68
    miniatures, 63–67
    simple shapes, 61–62
Shockley, Melanie Bentley,
    92, 139
Silicone molds, 53–54
Silver, purity of, 9
*Silver metal clay. See Art
    Clay Silver; Precious
    Metal Clay*
Silver metal paper, 15, 17,
    105–113
    beads, 111–112
    firing, 105
    gallery, 113
    paper punch, 106–107
    shaping, 108–110
    techniques for, 105
Silverware rings, 94–96
Simon, Barbara Becker, 11
Skinner blend, 123
Slip
    with fresh clay, 21
    gold, 100
    making, 22
    premixed, 15
    Syringe, 15, 22–23
Slow Dry clay, 16, 93
Soldering, 34
Spray bottle, for hydrating
    clay, 19, 20
Stainless steel brushes, 31

Stamps, texturing with,
    39, 42–43, 72
Stanley, Carl, 68, 134
Stone setting, 83–92
    bezel for, 84, 88–89
    firing with, 84–85
    gallery, 92
    pearls, 90–91
    rings, 97–98
Straws, 19, 73, 74
Strong, Carolee, 120
Super Sculpey, 50
Surface materials, 18
Syringe Type clay, 15, 22–23

T

Texturing, 38–44
    gallery, 44
    with stamps, 39, 42–43, 72
    tools, 19, 23, 38, 39
Thermocouple, 27
Thermoplastic, 49
Tools and supplies
    basic, 18–19
    sources for, 140–142
Toothpick, 18
Torch–firing, 28, 100, 105, 123
Tumbling, 32

U

Ultra Lite Beehive Kiln, 26, 27
Unfired clay
    finishing, 24–25
    repairs to, 25
Uroboros glass, 134

V

Valentine, Shahasp, 59, 99, 104
V–shaped cutting tool, 45,
    118, 122

W

Wakumoto, Candice, 77, 82
Workability, hydrating for, 20

X

X–Acto knife, 19, 57, 124

Z

Zirconia, 84, 97